Writing in Disguise

Academic Life

in

Subordination

Terry Caesar

OHIO UNIVERSITY PRESS

Athens

Ohio University Press, Athens, Ohio 45701
© 1998 by Terry Caesar
Printed in the United States of America
All rights reserved

Ohio University Press books are printed on acid-free paper ⊗ᵃ

02 01 00 99 98   5 4 3 2 1

Chapter 1 was first published in slightly different form as "Missionaries and Knots: Sexual Harassment" in *Centennial Review* 38 (Fall 1994). "The Green Bean Campaign in the Memo" was previously published in *New Literary History* 26 (Summer 1995).

Library of Congress Cataloging-in-Publication Data

Caesar, Terry
    Writing in disguise: academic life in subordination / Terry
Caesar.
        p.   cm.
    Includes bibliographical references (p.).
    ISBN 0-8214-1220-5 (cloth alk. paper)
    1. College Teaching—Psychological aspects. 2. College teachers—
Psychology. 3. Academic writing—Psychological aspects.
    I. Title.
    LB2331.C24 1998
    378.1'2'019—dc21   97-30432
                                                              CIP

Contents

Acknowledgments

I wish to thank three very different organizations. Two are professional. Without the assistance of the John Simon Guggenheim Memorial Foundation, I never would have had the time to write this book. I'm inexpressibly honored. Without the annual book award of the Northeast Modern Language Association (NEMLA), this book would never have been published. I'm profoundly grateful.

The third organization is familial—my in-laws. I want to recognize a number of them, ranging from my sister-in-law, Elzira Soares, who gave me the use of a special room as well as the pleasure of some unforgettable lunches, to my mother-in-law, Oscarina Bueno, who provided still more room and more food. *Gente que veio de Minas, feita de ouro sé.*

Finally, I want to thank my wife, Eva Bueno. She didn't suffer every moment of experience represented in this book. But she's provided the emotional intelligence that has enabled me to see every moment as worth trying to write about. Perhaps she will not be the only one to see how much this book is a haplessly disguised form of love for her.

Writing in Disguise

Writing and Disguise

1. Writing Inside Out

A publisher's representative once told me the following story. He knocked on a professor's office door. A loud sigh could be heard as he was invited in. The professor gestured for him to sit in an unusually soft chair, and he proceeded to lose his balance, bumping his head, hard, on a bookcase behind the chair. "Oh, dear," the professor exclaimed, "I suppose I'm going to have to use your textbook now!" After I had stopped laughing, the publisher's representative told me that, as it turned out, the professor didn't choose any books from the rep's list, and he added, "you know, the bastard didn't even ask for an examination copy."

You may not have to be an academic in order to find this story funny. You may only have to be someone for whom a text of some sort continually mediates, not to say defines, human relationships. Although the story comprehends much that is distinctive to academic life, including especially its reluctant concessions to the world outside the office door, what interests me here and in the following pages is the more general situation of people caught up in a certain kind of domination that results from

1

being normatively included in conditions of writing to which they can make no official protest. What do they do then, besides tell careful jokes?

My interest in this question is quite personal. In part the following pages are the result of a career predicated upon the subordination of subjectivity to institutional and disciplinary constraints about what merits expression in writing. The silence of someone who had better keep his mouth shut if he wants to sell a book is not exactly the same as the silence of someone who had better keep his mouth shut if he wants either to write a book or get it published. Yet for my purposes the differences between the two are far less important than their fundamental similarity, which is, in turn, the very condition of how writing in disguise gets produced when that which was silenced is expressed.

My own particular guise is an academic one, and I would present it as instructive because generally academics are adept at recreating what they do in words—but only if the terms have to do with ideals or issues. It must be emphasized at the outset that this book does not take that approach to the representation of academic life. Instead, I explore how the usual discourse of ideals or issues functions to prevent any other terms from coming into being. Indeed, one of the reasons academic life is so haunted by texts of all sorts is because there are simply no representational means available to so much criticism interior to this life, which must, therefore, conduct itself privately if at all.

Consider, for example, Catherine Stimpson, invited by the University of Michigan to give the third annual Davis-Markert-Nickerson lecture on the estimable subject of Academic and Intellectual Freedom. At the emotional center of her lecture is an autobiographical moment of the sort grown fashionable these days in literary studies. Stimpson relates the circumstances of the decision about her tenure, especially her outrage upon hearing that some of her male colleagues had openly engaged in sexual fantasies about her.

"Even now," Stimpson writes, "I cannot think of these scenes . . . without anger and shame. What was at stake was more than the freedom of my ideas and speech. My body was at stake. The dirty minds of my opponents were making my body dirty and then voting as if their speech were clean and cleansing."[1] Stimpson never leaves this scene, and returns to it directly in conclusion, by recounting the lawsuit she did not bring (the tenure verdict was "yes") and the public words she could not have spoken then against actions so safely private. Her lecture is in the deepest personal sense this public speaking at last. Academe hath no fury greater than that of a colleague scorned. The crucial consideration, however, is that the lecture be itself "clean." A mere airing of dirty laundry would appear far too grubby for the occasion.

My presentation of academic life begins and ends by focusing upon such low scenes of enduring personal incident because it is given only to the most eminent of the profession to speak in any way publicly about them. When eminences do speak in more personal terms, what usually results is an exhibition of why these terms do not abide very comfortably within those of professional constraint. By far the most remarkable recent performance is the lip-smacking invective against masochistic academics at a recent English Institute by Stanley Fish, whose rhetorical skills cannot quite refine away the apparently lived dimension of self-loathing. He concludes thus: "And finally I acknowledge that there is no justification whatever for [my own] performance, that it is irresponsible, self-indulgent, self-aggrandizing, and entirely without redeeming social or intellectual value. It is just something I have always wanted to do."[2]

What is remarkable about Fish's performance—which includes the following "aphorism": "academics like to eat shit, and in a pinch they don't care whose shit they eat"—is not only how it rehearses a species of contempt for academics normally consigned to the ignorant public. The contempt is severely circumscribed, if not usually suppressed, among academics themselves. We might well imagine, for example, what the newly tenured Stimpson said to her friends, and we can be even more certain that if she wrote anything about her enemies it was confined to letters to her friends. Academics are typical of subordinated groups in that it is virtually impossible for them to express some sort of personal outrage concerning business as usual. The burden of business as usual is in a very real sense to prevent such expression.

Consequently, I read the constitutive texts of the profession in terms of writing that can respond to them—or participate in them—only in the character of disguise. The following chapters examine the shaping force of what cannot be written, yet must be lived, upon what is. Ultimately, what must be lived *is* lived, at least in part, because it cannot be written. James Slevin has an essay in which he describes in careful political terms the hiring of a young professor by means of the usual series of official letters. In the course of explaining how his imaginary candidate is inscribed within a system of dispersed authority, with a provost at the top, he has the following footnote: "It is conceivable that [she] could be hired—and terminated six years later—by a man she will never meet. It is highly improbable that she and [the provost] will ever know one another."[3]

So, we might say, goes so much of modern life in all advanced industrial societies: we are both welcomed and dismissed by texts that have more authority in our lives than the people who write them, who don't even write them personally. What recourse do we ourselves have, when the same mode characterizes the replies we make? That is, what authority does the personal have if it must abide in a condition of subordination? What authority does it have if it comes into existence as a result of subordination?

The difference between the last two questions is important, and the following chapters are offered as explorations of the difference, if not the importance. Stories deliberately proliferate—jokes, anecdotes, fictions; in one respect, this book is about stories that don't get told, or valued, because others do instead. Parody occurs repeatedly; in another respect, this book is about the constitutive presence of parody in discourse of any sort. finally, I gradually emerge in my own right, as if to test the authority of autobiographical criticism itself, which is not so subordinated (or deprived) by what Charles Altieri terms "all the other analytic frameworks that contemporary intellectual life offers" that it cannot discover in these frameworks something of its own warrant.[4] The trick lies not so much in criticizing how this warrant has been denied as in demonstrating how it can be found, and then written out.

2. Further In

What would academic life look like if it were turned inside out? The answer I propose is that it would look like a series of texts, particularly including the letter Stimpson could never have presented as a lecture, or the lecture Fish would not have delivered as a letter. To say that most of these texts are intended to be read by a small, localized group of people only acts to limit (not to say literalize) how the example of last week's department minutes or last month's memo from the dean can be understood in broader terms that are not at all self-explanatory.

Even on the inside it is often difficult to so much as classify the wide variety of texts any academic institution generates and circulates daily. Some, such as minutes or memos, have more public character within an institution than others. In sharp contrast, sexual harassment is such a preeminent issue today (both inside and outside the academy) partially because the question of whether or not a case should have any public character at all is equivalent to the question of whether it should have any textual character. Some activity, on the other hand, such as anything to do with directing dissertations or resigning, is so institution-specific there is scarcely any need for it to attain textual form at all. Other activity, especially teaching, is highly monitored in similar ways at most institutions, and therefore represented variously in terms of faculty observation reports, student evaluations, committee summaries, and individual self-assessments.

What do most of these texts, so variously ephemeral, have in common? At least one thing: they are all embedded in an official discourse in which anything personal is potentially unsettling, provocative, and otherwise elusive of the sort of abstract, regulative official discourse in which the day-to-day business of an institution (or, in the case of rejection letters, a magazine) is normally represented.[5] Therefore, I cite in the following pages a still wider variety of texts, ranging from personal letters to novels, in order to study the more abstract relation between dominance and subordination. What interests me are the ways individuals come to terms, in writing, with the fact that they have to hear each year from the president about the budget crisis, or each month about the department's new curriculum, while from time to time they open envelopes to find that yet another article has been rejected or close classroom doors on still another semester's classes about which they would scarcely know what to write if they could.

My view of academic life is based on conflict—not only between professors and administrators or between teaching and research but between experience as lived and experience as represented. Conflict is constitutive of even the most mundane texts, as in the English department minutes of Forest Park Community College in St. Louis that Richard Ohmann cites at the conclusion of a chapter in his pioneering study, *English in America*:

> The meeting was adjourned by the skillful, reasonable, and courageous Garger, who, even though wearied of carrying heavy burdens of responsibility on his sturdy, though narrow, shoulders, remains ever ready to serve the arrogant wishes and base desires of the members of the English department,

Writing Lab and GC people, Humanities Division generally, the Junior College Board of Trustees, the vast hierarchical plethora of Administrators, Deans, sub-deans, minor administrators, the tax-payers of St. Louis and St. Louis County, the Nixon Administration, the Joint Chiefs of Staff, the Board of Directors of the recently aligned (or is it exposed) United Fund, my near and distant blood relatives, and humanity generally. Maybe even students.[6]

My point is not that such a document is at all formally typical of departmental minutes. I merely want to remark upon how easily, simply by virtue of a subjective gesture, the entire educational project is transformed into a hapless linkage of competing aims, disparate groups, and subordinated constituencies. If we concede (as even minor administrators probably would) that such a perception of its own purpose is probably inescapable in the life of any professional unit on occasion, the important thing is that a certain fatigued moment about the whole enterprise be presented as frivolous — and therefore still committed. If instead the moment could be given directly and in its own name, what name would it have? What would minutes be that were not minutes, and who would be authorized to write them? One might as well ask what name to give education that is not education.

In other words, the danger of this sort of subordinated writing is not so much, I think, that the illusion of professional consensus might be shattered. The danger seems to me to be that the stable form of the public transcript itself could be subverted by indistinct private energies. Therefore, the public transcript demands compliance, and tolerates resistance only when carefully recreated as a form of compliance, "ever ready to serve," as written above. Let me give a more personal example, where resistance is at once less compliant and therefore less public.

A while ago one of the best students to graduate in recent years from my department's small graduate program was found to have taken the same course twice. Even if the content was quite different (as I knew, since the course was mine), the number was listed the same in her transcript, and this was against the rules. What to do? She was a friend. While the department temporized, I decided to write her a letter, from which I give the first two paragraphs:

> I regret to inform you that an aberration has been discovered in your transcript. It seems you received credit for twice taking the same graduate course, English 509, Literary Theory. This should not have occurred, er, in theory.

The fact that it did in, well, practice, does not excuse a not insignificant stain on the integrity of our graduate requirements in our largest program.

Consequently I must request that you present yourself in the English department lounge during the first three weeks of this semester, at a time jointly agreed upon by you, the English chair, your advisor, and the [building] custodian. At that time you will be required to relinquish exactly half of your theories. Deconstruction, feminism—it matters not which ones, or any one, as long as you are theoretically bereft by half when you leave the lounge (and please don't forget to turn off the coffee machine). One of the English 509 courses must be purged from your record, and of course it is unfortunate that this must be accomplished at the cost of purging half your mind.

I signed the letter as the dean of the Graduate School. At the time, I was the departmental coordinator of the graduate program. As usual, I was not comfortable in the position when it came to enforcing the rules. So the way I found I could extricate myself from the responsibility of having to do so anyway in this instance was to displace my authority, exaggerate, and then mock it. I thought the student would be amused. Alas, a friend of hers told me she turned white upon first reading the letter. Then I realized that once again in my career I had written an example of what James Scott terms "the often fugitive political conduct of subordinate groups."[7]

Scott's whole comprehension of such conduct is important to me. Each of the succeeding chapters deliberately makes some reference to his work. In one respect, this book constitutes an academic rereading of Scott. For example, what the above letter exemplifies, I believe, is a scrambling of his two basic textual categories: a "hidden transcript," in the guise (and from the position) of a public transcript. Unlike the groups that Scott studies, such as slaves, professors are distinguished by their ability to read the public transcript of administrators very acutely. Both know the realities and the limits of its power.[8] I could have sent a copy of the letter to the dean himself, and he would probably have laughed, if more guardedly than I may have liked. We would both know that, regrettably or not, there abide formalities that include us both.

I did not send him a copy because then the letter would have become too public. In order for it to keep its edge, I judged it would have to remain private, or hidden. Scott's hidden transcripts work this way. They circulate only among friends and initiates, or between people who can take their mutual marginalization or exclusion for granted. The student, I assumed, knew that in some sense I *was*, in effect, forced to play the role of the dean. "While the hidden transcript cannot be described as the truth that contradicts the lies told to power," Scott states, "it is correct to say that the hidden transcript is a self-disclosure that power relations normally exclude from the official transcript."[9] But there are even more complicated ways of disclosing oneself, or of hiding.

These ways are what you get when you try to study how academic life can be turned inside out. How often does somebody in a department give the official record of the last meeting a joking inflection, or does somebody else take hold of an official transcript for reasons that are still more personal? It is impossible to say. It might be necessary to add that of course academics are not the only ones who do this. Many in all sorts of large organizations undoubtedly produce hidden transcripts, as a function of having been charged to enact repeated ceremonies of what Scott terms "discursive affirmation from below."[10] If so, we need to ask at this point how academics differ.

One venerable *topos* of most professional groups is the self-evaluation. Let me give a couple of paragraphs from the report of a friend of mine in the diplomatic service. He purports to write to the "Ratings Officer" directly about himself, inviting this personage to collude with him in hopes that they will both receive comfortable pensions.

> While his repulsive appearance suggests considerable miscegenation or worse in his background, O. remains Irish enough to drink heavily and suffer the psychopathologies common among products of parochial schools and Jesuit universities. The RMO considers these problems hopeless but O. has not let them interfere with the little bit of work he has done. Indeed, the USG might have been better served had this officer drunk even more heavily: he was reportedly sober when programming an American economist at the School of Fine Arts on a Sunday morning, and when he published a letter in "Il Mattino" defending indicted Italian politicians on the basis that "a nation of thieves deserves no better."
>
> Substantive Knowledge/Independent Judgment. It is true that the officer displays some familiarity with recent changes in U.S. social attitudes. But telling people he remembers "when women knew their place" contributes minimally to CP objectives. Nonetheless, that he made this comment also in the presence of the previous PAO, a female officer, suggests a certain willingness to express dissenting views.

Such a self-evaluation, I think, is the consequence of so many previous discursive affirmations that the bonds of compliance can be felt even in the resistance. In this sense my friend is no different than any academic, subject to various organizational pieties, behavioral objectives, and politically correct attitudes. The crucial difference is this: while a diplomat may enjoy as many textual occasions as a professor, he is not subject to the same expectations about what he writes. His writing—a brief introduction of a distinguished speaker, or a long report on a fact-finding mission—is so-to-speak more *immanent*. I am thinking of a particularly trenchant remark by Reed Way Dasenbrock in a review of two recent books on the profession of English: "I see many reasons besides professional self-interest—though that is certainly involved—for resisting the notion that our professional traditions have value only as a spur to their transcendence."[11]

Undoubtedly diplomacy is heir to its own traditions. I do doubt, though, that these traditions (or those of any other professional organization or community) countenance transcendence of normal practice in the way the teaching profession does, where the way to transcendence is through writing, not teaching; Dasenbrock cites one of his books on how professors invariably describe a writing or a research project when asked what they are working on. Hence, my unremitting concentration upon the failure of writing in an academic career to afford transcendence from daily circumstances in which (notwithstanding professional traditions to the contrary) nothing more than teaching is expected.

In the following pages, the letter that should not be written is all of a piece to me with the article that could not be published. Each is founded upon the personal story that I cannot quite tell, except to represent it as a story—at once theoretical and anecdotal—about hidden transcripts. Once, many years ago, I received a formal letter of acceptance from the head of a conference session to whom I'd submitted a paper. Well and good. But on the back of the letter the man's colleague (whose opinion had apparently been consulted) had written that he saw no reason my paper could not be accepted because, though it said nothing new, it "wouldn't do any harm." I wrote the session head an angry letter. He wrote back that it was "unprofessional" of me. Academics like this word. Deans aren't the only ones who use it. I should have written a more creative letter, and contemplated a more provocative destination.

3. Writing Out

Let me give a more extended example of just such creativity, based on another conference. Or rather, another sort of conference, the kind you are invited to attend in order to listen to an all-star lineup of featured speakers. Such conferences can give rise to a number of troubling emotions, depending upon how trendy the subject or how submerged in your own job the speakers make you feel. In the case of my friend, who wrote the letter, the situation was further complicated by the fact that she learned of the conference from a brochure included with the rejection form letter she received some months after applying for a Women's Studies position at Purdue.

The letter congratulated itself on the fact that more than six hundred applications had been received for the position. The brochure announced a symposium on "Feminism and Multiculturalism," and proudly listed speakers with such impressively multicultural names as Shahrzad Mojab, Yi-Ling Ru, and Banu Subramaniam. My friend was particularly struck by one Beth Brant, identified as "Bay of Quinte Mohawk writer and activist on Native American and lesbian issues, mom and grandmother." She decided to write the following letter to the Director of Women's Studies, which I give in full:

> Your letter of February 18 shocked and disturbed me. Not as a notification about the Women's Studies position; after all, to hear about the 600 applicants the position drew is to be humbled by their sheer number and my own insignificance. The Symposium, however, is a completely different thing. Upon reading the names and qualifications of your participants, I was absolutely enraged.
>
> How could you have disdained such a crucial constituency as the one I represent? I don't know whether to address your blatant sexism, ethnicism, chauvinism, preferentialism, biologism, and general degraded humanism, or to simply turn away in disgust. As a Brazilian bisexual mother involved in the critique of the subject as the object of science, I protest.
>
> Of course you have your obligatory workshops on multicultural issues, but all of them are shot through by Pan-American effacement, heterosexual monologism and maternal disempowerment. Where is the space for those of us who are not dykes, nor fykes, nor whatever else the fashionable name is, but who profess a deep commitment to the globalization of instinctual politics from a South American matrix?
>
> I will keep you no longer. Of course I wish good luck to you and the per-

sons invited for the position at your Program. As for the Symposium, as long as you keep it so disingenuously heterogeneous, count me out, as I am anyway, once more.

Once again, I do not know quite how to classify such a letter in terms of Scott's paradigm, although the paradigm discloses its peculiar relevance. Unlike my earlier letter to the student, the one above has a public dimension because it is not written to a friend. And yet it is written out of private motives not wholly represented (or understood) in public form. Does the first circumstance explain why the letter brought her no reply or acknowledgment from Women's Studies? Does the second explain why, when my friend sent a copy to a gay friend of hers, he wrote back quite seriously angry because she had not told him that she was bisexual? My sense is that any writing from a subjugated position is almost inevitably fraught with such ambiguities, whether or not the words are communicated as a hidden transcript.

Why write such a letter in the first place? It is one thing to say that someone who does wants to be a featured speaker too. It is another to say that someone who does knows she will never be featured, whether because lacking the best institutional clout, the right multicultural identity, or the most wholehearted commitment to having a career that partakes so generously of dominant positions.[12] Often it merely has to do with publishing a book. One reason Frank Lentricchia, for example, can openly fret about whether his autobiographical inclinations are "just so much self indulgence" is because they are represented in one book—published, moreover, at the same time as a more conventional and scholarly one.[13] Some self-indulgence is sanctioned to be so, just as some disguises are.

Lately Robert Hughes has stated that "most contact between academe and the general intelligent reader seems to have withered, because over-specialization and the *deformations professionnelles* of academic careerism are killing it off."[14] Undoubtedly so. But academic life takes more forms than either Hughes or the general reader realizes. One form is based on resistance—ultimately, I think, to any particular form at all. Of course it makes a difference whether your objection is to the routine affirmations of yet another department meeting or to those of a fashionably new conference on multiculturalism. But how much of a difference?

Institutional practices are sometimes in contradiction with ideological ones. At other times the two have nothing much to do with each other at all.

People usually write hidden transcripts for highly contingent reasons, and perhaps all that can ultimately be claimed for these texts is that they exemplify, in Charles Altieri's words, a "kind of activity whose mode of inhabiting subjection undoes its authority by demonstrating the angers and anxieties that are the conditions it imposes as the price for being its subject."[15]

I don't mean to presume that you are such a subject only if you are an academic. Patricia Williams, for example, has an essay about the hopelessness of trying to represent her rage at an incident of racial discrimination. She engages in a series of writings: in her journal, on a poster, and finally for a symposium sponsored by a law review. What happens is that first the name of the clothing store in question, and then her race, are edited out of the article to be published by the review. Williams tells the story all over again (concentrating this time on the "ideology" of the law review editing process) at another conference — only to find herself wildly misrepresented in a newspaper account.[16] Sometimes there is no more consolation for having to inhabit subjection than there is for having to be alive.

For an academic, however, whose career ultimately will be assessed in terms of how self-presentation is managed in writing, the matter of subjection is quite distinctly exacerbated. What Hughes appears to assume, along with many outside academic life, is that any individual is free to shape his or her career, including the fact that you can write what you like. With luck — for example, the right friends — you can have a career in which your personal life is happily at one with your professional life, and your professional life can be expressed as a vision of fundamental developments in the profession itself. "In 1981 I got tenure," Jane Gallop concludes in the introduction to her latest book. "Around the same time, American feminist literary criticism entered the heart of a contradiction."[17] She mentions at the outset how her career (not to say her fame) was effectively born when she was asked to write a response in one of the most distinguished journals in the field.

The account of academic life in the following chapters is what you get when nobody asks — or when you are simply not in position to speak to any symposium or to contribute to any journal, distinguished or not. Hughes to the contrary, the deformations of "careerism" are not for most. (And, as Gerald Graff remarks, "if the academic humanities are *over*-anything, they are *over*-generalized rather than overspecialized.")[18] You may, for example, write what you like. But you will quickly discover if you try to get what you have written published, just as Williams does, that it had better accord with professional norms—a fact you should have learned already while writing a dissertation. And what about the writing of a dissertation? Why precisely does it appear to be taken for granted?

The institutional, ideological, or personal character of what subjugates you as an academic while writing a dissertation is of course not perfectly symmetrical with what subjugates you, later, while writing an article—whether or not you have to publish it in order to receive tenure or promotion. From the outside, it is always possible to make distinctions.[19] Inside, I believe the imperative to write a dissertation and to write an article feels continuous enough, at least enough for anyone to write some sort of hidden transcript about the imperative. Of course such a transcript can always be viewed as an instance of aborted politics. (My friend above, for example, could have written a more direct letter, or even have attended the conference in order to make her views known.) I would prefer to view a hidden transcript instead as being about something where politics has already failed, if indeed political activity ever could have been made manifest at all. If you are going to express a dissent against the whole framework supporting the writing of dissertations, you do not necessarily want to mount a campaign, much less (somewhat ironically) plan a paper on the subject for a conference.

Scott terms the "logic of disguise" of hidden transcripts to be one of "infrapolitics." He explains: "Because open political activity is all but precluded, resistance is confined to the informal networks of kin, neighbors, friends and community rather than formal organizations."[20] It is important to be clear about what is being precluded. Policy issues are debated all the time in higher education. Conferences are full of issues. Memos strive to implement them. Therefore, one can easily form the impression that such debate stands in for the range and extent of discussion on all other matters. It does not. The public transcript fails to comprehend the whole range and extent of attitudes about policy issues alone, although, since the dominant writes the script (for this is Scott's point), some expressions of feeling cannot be known at all except in secret or in disguise because they are too personal.

In other words, the public domain itself provides the closure against which (and within which) hidden transcripts operate. To define the boundaries of this domain in too systematic or thorough a manner only makes the transcripts more political than they aspire to be (as well as the public domain more static). Examples I have already cited do not aim to be political. Nor do the ones I cite in the following chapters, which, similarly, either continue the logic of disguise into a public occasion or else avoid this occasion, albeit sometimes just barely. My peculiar view of academic life is that its inside is made up of failed outsides. That is why this book is deliberately structured so that it gets progressively more personal, beginning with a public writing viewed at its most inward and concluding with a private writing made public.

In the public transcript, failure of any sort hardly ever resonates—virtually by definition; Catherine Stimpson's tenure bid—for all her anguish—is successful. Let me give another example. Nancy Miller has an essay on her career in which she mentions at one point that she wrote the epilogue to her first book (based on her dissertation) "in a single sitting, in rage against an anonymous and extremely hostile (female) reader's report. I wish—or I think I wish—I still had a copy of the report."[21] I, too, wish she had, and that she had quoted from it, so we could see one example of how what Scott refers to as "closure" operates.

If we inquire into the reasons why such reports are never quoted in print, I think we can be content with a simple answer: to dwell on readers' reports is to dwell on failure. Miller doesn't say how she managed to get the book published when it had merited such a hostile report. (Was it produced for an earlier press? Or was there another report more favorable—and then a third that concurred?) But she did get the book published. Her response to the reader may have been invested with as many personal energies as a hidden transcript. However, her occasion in the essay is now public. She can mention the reader's report because she succeeded. There is no danger of an accusation of sour grapes.

How many people, though, cannot mention these reports because the book was never published? For an academic, failure to publish your dissertation may be the most decisive fact in a whole career—affecting whether you get tenure, how long you stay at your first job, or how likely it is you can move on to another. Whether or not you are more enraged than Miller, you will not learn who wrote a report. A reader normally writes one in his or her own disguise. Unlike a hidden transcript, the report is anonymously embedded in a formal professional network. Consequently, an academic less fortunate than Miller who receives an unfavorable report has, finally, only the consolation of a personal, informal network within which to write a response. Who else would want to read it? The public transcript authorizes no one, not even the director of the press that called for the report in the first place.

Indeed, this is the trouble with the public transcript even when its author is known, and works in the same department with you. Suppose we consider a more mundane affair: how to object to a colleague's conclusions after a teaching observation? The person who makes the observation, and then writes the report, does so in his or her own name. Faculty in hundreds of departments at universities across the United States are obliged, either through administrative directives or union contracts, to write these reports. Seldom is anybody who is observed obliged to do anything more than sign a report after reading it. But what to do if the report is not favorable?

If in teaching, unlike publishing, there is some textual space for self-defense, its status is nevertheless so unclear that individuals rarely write one. (Virtually never if they are part-time teachers.) Why? Somewhat paradoxically, I think "observees" sense the same thing that "rejectees" feel after reading a reader's report: what they could write would only be personal — or rather, be perceived as personal. And in this situation "personal" means, as it usually does in an academic context, "too" personal. Just so, the reason the observation will always be accorded more textual weight is that it will not be taken as too personal, no matter that it's personally signed. What counts as "personal?" Not some ontological definition, but merely a structural one. The observee is *in position* to be personal, whereas the observer is not, and therefore partakes of the anonymous authority of the reader of a manuscript.

"If there is an academic type of statement," Sande Cohen writes, "it may well be close to the composition of judicial/legal pronouncements, embeddings, in which complex and recalcitrant materials are subjected to an *incorporeal* transformation, as when a biographical reference turns a document into an 'accused' simultaneously processed as a member of the idiotic couple, 'innocent/guilty.' "[22] The fact of an immanent legality as a formal quality of academic language may be illustrated nowhere better than in reports of teaching observations. If you are somehow "accused," the transcript is not ultimately designed to acknowledge your own textual response at all, except as an unfortunately "corporeal" manifestation.

So better to avoid being accused. Cohen has another provocative claim:

"Is it not fair to say that a very real part of an 'academic thing' (as impersonal object) is precisely this horror of what Deleuze calls, after Kafka, the 'absolute practical necessity' of having to defend oneself in every manner possible?"[23] Probably not. Practical necessities are seldom fair. But if you are going to have to defend yourself, in a sense, absolutely and at all times, you had better already have tried to affect the sort of "incorporeal" transformation the lack of which might bring you under attack in the first place. In academic terms, one way to do it is not writing anything at all except insofar as it accords with the public transcript, even when the person who writes it, and writes it critically about *you*, has an office just down the hall.

4. In Disguise

I hate writing teaching observation reports because they consist of nothing else but public transcript. Once a friend and I fooled around with a form that managed to bypass the report as *writing*. The two and a half pages consisted of the following sort of thing:

The weather was
___ fine
___ stormy
___ not fine
___ absent
___ typical

Throughout the class, it was
___ evident
___ not evident
___ semi-evident
___ clear
___ absolutely unspecified

that
___ the students
___ the teacher
___ neither
___ both

experienced

___ rapport

___ jouissance

___ community

___ fatigue

___ none of the above

This ___ observer

     ___ observeress

felt

___ the students

___ silly

___ empowered

___ obsessed

___ superfluous

___ ridiculous

___ aporetic

___ apologetic

___ pedagogic

___ contractually bound.

But we never tried to use this form. Perhaps we should have. You can never be completely sure that what Michel de Certeau terms "operational schemas" cannot be somehow absorbed in a "field," in order to become "something like a second level interwoven into the first," and thereby create "a certain play in the machine through a stratification of different and interfering kinds of functioning."[24] At the time, though, it seemed to suffice that we had just written something *out*. Other than the academy, does any other kind of organization in which you customarily have to produce something in writing result in so much concurrent writing that can only be shown, if at all, in disguise?

Not long ago I wrote a report based on the observation of an unusually interesting class, co-taught by two new members of the department. I hardly knew them. Our chair told me they were especially anxious to have people attend their class because of its "experimental" nature. Indeed, the role-playing I saw proved so stimulating that I produced the longest report I have ever written, praising some aspects of the class, criticizing others, quoting Louis Althusser on ideology, and expiring thus:

Alas, and in conclusion, this teaching observation report, no matter how different itself, only functions as the same as all the rest. I've spent nearly two hours writing it. I could have spent fifteen minutes. Once again I want to record how empty the writing and the routinizing of these reports has become, how overcome with unconscious assumptions and unasked questions (e.g., who am I to write this report in the first place?), how *imaginary* in Althusser's rather exacting sense. Did somebody say ideology? The "real" subject of these reports may not be, as I think myself, the political need for departmental consensus and unity. But, in any case, there's too much of what I can only term the real that never gets into these reports, and my _____ at having to do them anymore is so real as to be beyond both fantasy and representation.

I have been writing a last paragraph similar to this for the past few years. No one has ever spoken to me to me about it. The reports have come to seem so vacant I sometimes convince myself that I've managed to disappear. Above, the absent word _____ functions, I suppose, as a sign of my own absence, and no matter that the preceding pages are flush with my presence in the form of jibes, jokes, impressions, and speculations. This time I expected my new colleagues to attest to the fact that they had "read and discussed" the report with me (as they are contractually bound to do) by signing it. Few actually discuss anymore. Everybody signs.

So I was surprised when weeks passed, and the secretary failed to present to me the report so I could sign in turn. Had something happened? But what? The secretary confirmed that she had both retyped my report and given it to the two teachers, according to procedure. More weeks passed. I never spoke to either one, nor either one to me. We had barely spoken before. Had they refused to sign the report now and perhaps convinced someone else to write another instead? How much did I care? The other reason I failed to inquire further is that I hoped the whole system was somehow collapsing.

It was not. When I learned during the next semester that I had been assigned to observe one of the same two teachers, I balked, and wrote a letter to the chair refusing to do it, especially because my observee-to-be had disdained to so much as acknowledge the previous semester's observation. This turned out to be the first the chair had known about it. When he spoke to the co-teachers, they claimed they had never seen my observation report. The chair told me he had no interest in pursuing such a blatant lie. Rather than explore what the whole incident disclosed about the observation system, he was more emphatic about one point: having to do an observation was a "contract issue." "You could be fired," he assured me.

So I complied. Further resistance was futile. I have always preferred to resign (see my last chapter) rather than be fired. Although a few days later I stayed in my observee's class for only five minutes, I assumed the role of observer once more, and in ten or fifteen minutes produced a requisite script. Eventually, you have to, no matter how you strive to mock, parody, or otherwise play with it. Much as I would like to demonstrate in the following pages how triumphantly such requisite scripts can be transformed or overcome, I don't. My reader will find here little of what Candace Lang has termed "the rebellious, Promethean potential of autobiographical writing to destabilize traditional authority and to transform the self over and against that authority."[25]

It is the nature of the peculiar authority examined here that the self subordinate under it should perforce be more circumspect, devious, and even ultimately faithful. Granted, as Altieri mentions, "autobiographical criticism gravitates toward alienation stories."[26] But this doesn't mean that the same story is fated to be retold about the personal energies hopelessly "in" subordination just because they're personal. Each of the following chapters challenges this fate in various ways, and in the above instance, I believe, a personal response *as such* on my part was impossible. In order to write at all I had to appear in disguise—void, blank—and therefore to suffer the divisions of disguise. Consequently, I would have my observation story disclose two other things that swerve away from the alienation plot. If one thing is more private than the other, each discloses something no less important about the deepest divisions of academic life. The first has to do with students, while the second is about resignation.

Although I have a penultimate chapter on teaching, students are not very important to the vision of academic endeavor proposed by this book. In a sense, I suppose, this is necessarily so, if you're going to concentrate instead on the difficulty of writing about directing dissertations or getting rejected for publication. But such necessity expresses a wider assumption: I don't think the most significant features of an academic's career usually have to do with students in any specific way. (Unless you marry one.)

Instead, just as in the above story about classroom observation, students figure collectively, in the background, as a pretext rather than the text itself, which is written by colleagues, and then taken up by the institutional structure in ways still more remote from the classroom.

The claim could be put differently: students have to do with the hidden transcript, not the public one; I have already given an example from my own experience. Insofar as the public transcript is concerned, teaching has been a great source of dissatisfaction for me because it has been another thing I've never been able to make public through writing. (See chapter 5.) Of course hardly anybody else does. Unless the experience is especially peculiar and distinctive, the public record about teaching experience either draws on some strictly personal eminence founded upon scholarship or else feeds so smoothly into available public concerns that the personal basis is stretched too wide to make much sense.[27]

Rhetoric concerning teaching of course varies from country to country. I wrote this book while living in Brazil, where the teaching of a college professor generally is not subordinated, through the prestige of research, to the greater value of writing. Nor, I believe (and largely for this reason), could the sorts of hidden transcripts I study acquire the same degree and kind of public implication in Brazil. Specific institutional or cultural differences between the two countries are deliberately mentioned in each chapter here because such differences have helped shape my whole sense of what it is to be an academic. Compared to the United States, the whole disparity between dominant and subordinate in higher education is much greater in Brazil. And yet, very little of the writing in disguise I examine would be plausible, let alone possible, to Brazilians, unless it were wholly infrapolitical, as it probably is.

Why is this so? Much of the reason has to do with the fact that, since overt political activity is far more common among Brazilian professors, writing displaces more political energies for American academics than it does for Brazilians — especially the personal, vagrant sort of writing that interests me throughout. In Brazil, subordinated writing of any kind would be more politically charged than it is in the United States. Depending upon the ideological climate, the slightest parody might be a potent political act. You have to be careful because it is not only in the dean's office that files are kept. In the United States, on the other hand, you can afford to be more frivolous and careless. I don't agree with Sande Cohen: "The institution called academe will not contribute to the problematizing of its own practices."[28] Problematizing happens all the time within American universities. What does not happen all the time is that each bit of activity gets—to use one of Cohen's favored terms—politically "coded." First it has to get known; the scope of a personal letter or a hidden transcript is too restricted, and stays restricted.[29]

Emphasizing national difference helps me to explain why, although (as I examine in my last chapter) I once wrote no less than two letters of resignation, one was too single-minded in its politics, and the other too careless. It was too easy for me to write them. As an agent, I could have it both ways—performing a political act in one country, while just writing "something" with respect to another country. Edward Said has a fine sentiment: "A single overmastering identity at the core of the academic enterprise, whether that identity be Western, African, or Asian, is a confinement, a deprivation."[30] But you still have to be careful, and you can live in only one country at a time. The same democratic license that made it possible for the model of such a letter to be political also made it possible for it to be evacuated of politics—and vice versa. It would have been less disingenuous, I think, if I had just resigned, and not written anything. But then I would not have been the American academic that I was, and remain.

Once I met a woman in Brazil who told me that she must have resigned from ten jobs (mostly the sort of part-time employment so common to Brazilian professors) in her life. But she never once wrote a letter of resignation. Could I likely meet someone in the United States who would state the same thing? I doubt it. Americans participate in a cultural pact whereby to write a text to accompany the act is already to experience the logic through which the text can become the act itself. The logic is as peculiar to Americans as sending greeting cards to stand for friendship, much less writing letters to the editor to signify political action. In writing letters of resignation, I took myself to have resigned.

Academic terms are never purely academic. Academic life is inseparably part of American life, if only, as David Bromwich repeatedly emphasizes throughout *Politics by Other Means*, so that it can function as the symbol of a self-enclosed community where the ravages of the larger society might be healed. Yet if the academy could be so impossibly isolated, as so many defenders and reformers envision it to be, I would offer my letters of resignation as testimony to how thoroughly teaching, the central activity in higher education, suffers a division from itself with respect to writing. My own career has been an expression of this division, and has not been institutionally situated to take advantage of it. Even when I wanted to quit teaching, I wrote about it instead, and of course wrote in disguise.

Missionaries and Knots

in Sexual Harassment

In Edward Allen's recent academic novel, *Mustang Sally*, the hero, a professor, Packard Schmidt, tells a joke in class about a woman who asks a man to give her a seat on the bus because she's pregnant. When the man asks her how long she's been pregnant, she looks at her watch and says, "About forty-five minutes." Students in the class file a written complaint, charging sexual harassment. The text of this complaint is not given in the novel. Subsequently, our hero has little choice but to write a letter of apology to the student newspaper. This letter is printed in the novel; it characterizes the "incident" as "regrettable" and "ill-advised," thanks the students for pointing out its offensiveness, and affirms that the college "ideal of community" must come before free speech or humor.[1]

The structure of sexual harassment in academic life works very much like this, although seldom with such admirable closure. First, something happens. In the above case, it is something spoken. Then it gets recreated in writing—most commonly, in the form of a complaint either written by the aggrieved party or on her behalf. More writing follows. If a legal proceeding ensues, the writing can swell to enormous proportions, especially in the case of counter-charges. I know of a small department at a small university where the entire department filed a libel suit against one member, who had filed no fewer than four charges of sexual harassment with the administration, two involving members of her department.

One of these four charges arose from when the woman was explaining a previous charge to one of her colleagues. It had to do with how a first-year student repeatedly mispronounced a word in French so that it became obscene. Her colleague said that it was absurd to attribute sexual harassment to the student, who was ignorant of the mistake. He gave a corresponding example in Spanish of the same sort of common error. Thereupon his colleague left, and filed a charge of sexual harassment against him as well.

I mention advisedly a true story perhaps more comic than Allen's fictional one. In each case, the filing of a charge opens up a gap between the apparent triviality of original event and the seriousness of its ethical or legal meaning. Furthermore, in each case the status of something spoken is subsequently restated in terms of the authority of something written. In Allen's novel, the only way to contend with this authority (poor Packard mentions eight hundred wasted dollars spent on a lawyer) is eventually to rewrite it yet again in the form of a public letter.[2]

What I contend about sexual harassment is that the subject has to do with a recurrent conflict in American academic life between private, or hidden, experience and its public presentation. Of course this conflict is neither limited to academic life, nor is its specific content over each decade or generation set exclusively by academic conditions; without the Clarence Thomas–Anita Hill hearings of 1991 the power of sexual harassment as an academic issue today is probably unimaginable. However, no other setting brings out its peculiar nuances quite so well. Universities are much closer to their respective communities than federal bureaucracies, for example (even when institutions are so large—or public—that a distinction seems idle). Moreover, possible scandal or legal action affects the very identity of the institution. The above department filed its libel suit because the administration feared publicity in taking any action against the woman, and set aside the department's decision against rehiring her.

In some cases, such as flagrant abuses of responsibility by dissertation directors, the bureaucratic order can keep private experience private by containing the kind of text that can be initiated on its basis. In other instances, such as public reports or memos, private experience can be accorded space for textual representation, circulation and even play. Sexual harassment, however, presents an enormous challenge to academic structures because the whole subject of sex is prey to so much innuendo, rumor, misunderstanding, and provocation of all sorts. Or to put it another way, sex is so *private*. Academics may have sex. But it must not be the result of any kind of harassment.[3] And, except in fiction, they should not write about it.

Bureaucracies, however, can. The official solution to the threat of sex is to cast it as publicly accountable—at least sex between students and professors. Universities such as the College of William and Mary or Oberlin College, which effectively ban sex between students and professors in virtually all cases, have been widely criticized because the policies would be unenforceable. But one can argue that this is not their intent. A legal ban has the effect of making sex already written, and therefore removed from the private realm, where, in a sense, it could formerly only have taken place because no public moment had been written into it.

I want to argue that the discourse of sexual harassment authorizes the writing of this moment, enabling the continuous characterization of an action as sexual, and then the conversion of the presence of sex into a complaint about harassment. The conditions are not easy to study because only the public transcript makes specific conditions available at all. The only other sources of information are fiction and anecdote. People who commit sexual harassment don't write about it. If the above letter from *Mustang Sally* written by a real Packard Schmidt appeared in a real campus newspaper, no one would have any more information about the "incident" (and learn nothing about the joke). Just so, few people may ever learn anything about the extremely complicated, inward nature of the charges and counter-charges in one department of one university.

Professors or students who commit sexual acts together do, on the other hand, occasionally write about it; I want to conclude this chapter with a discussion of an unusually provocative article by Jane Gallop. The fact, though, that this is not an auspicious time in American higher education to try to tell true stories about the existence of sexuality raises the following question: what can be *known* about any one sexual occasion? The discourse of sexual harassment now sets the terms. Most institutions are in a position to deploy an impressive amount of general information. In a ten-page booklet of Policies and Procedures on Sexual Harassment, my own university defines the offense, stipulates an Advisory Panel, describes informal and formal methods of resolution, and lists a number of relevant state agencies. Yet one reads this document (from which I will later quote) with a sense that many stories simply cannot be told. The question of what can be known about sex has gotten mixed up with the question of what can be stipulated about sexual harassment.

How can we explain this development, at least in an academic context? American institutions resolute for the latest progressive policies now find themselves in position to be exploring the whole status of the erotic in academic life—or rather, and more scandalously, the inextricability of institutional relations, social relations, and sexual relations. If the discourse of sexual harassment has been burdened to make these relations extricable, publicly accountable, and impeccably textual, I believe there is at least one thing that has fatefully remained repressed: academic life as erotic. Or, if not erotic, a structure from which the erotic cannot be extricated because exactly the same things make for academic organization and value as make for sexual provocation and opportunity. The rest is private, and should be upheld as private.

But first it is necessary to understand how utterly American is this transposition of private energies into public pieties.

&

In her introduction to the second edition of *The Lecherous Professor,* one of the first studies of sexual harassment on campus, one of the authors, Billie Wright Dziech, concludes by, in effect, initiating a brief dialogue with harassers and their defenders. Most "disturbing" from among the mail she has received is a long letter from "an engineering professor in Arizona," who winds up impugning Dziech's motives for writing by comparing her to a prostitute, and then quoting a colleague of his who characterizes writers who take up "RIGHT CAUSES" thus: "It is a bit like the missionaries that went to Hawaii to 'do good.' They did very well indeed and ended up taking the whole island away from the natives."[4]

Dziech defends herself by pointing out that the book has not made her rich, and that she had tenure before she wrote it. More important, she is convinced of two things: the authors' cause is the right one and their attempt has been to keep "the island" in the possession of those who know it best. But in opening up just enough of her own study to another voice, Dziech discloses two things about the text: her principles can be contested, and her whole discourse can be seen as a parochial one.

Of course few social issues have become more quickly and universally recognized, not to say honored, in the academy during the last decade. That anyone anywhere could now write a *defense* of sexual harassment seems unthinkable. Therefore, however, the subject has become an excellent example of what James Scott has studied as the public transcript, which always constitutes a writing of the dominant over against the subordinate. The dynamics of power between the two groups are not simple. Conflict is not prevented, only structured. Scott at one point defines dominant discourse thus: "a plastic idiom or dialect that is capable of carrying an enormous variety of meanings, including those that are subversive of their use as intended by the dominant."[5]

Of course the letter from the Arizona professor is scarcely subversive, in Scott's full sense. How to estimate the representative status of one letter, or to infer some larger and more resonant politics on the basis of it? All we can judge is that conflict exists in the form of a "hidden transcript" from the same social site that Dziech claims to master. We can say little about the status of this transcript, other than that it discloses Dziech's text to be in a relation of power against it, and not simply of truth, notwithstanding Dziech's own protestations of truth to the contrary.

The letter does suggest one thing about the source of this power: it is foreign to the country in question. Of course, whether a college campus is in any way comparable to Hawaii (with its suggestions of sexy South Sea freedom) *is* the question *The Lecherous Professor* is anxious to deny. Accepting the analogy is to accept the possibility for sex, not to say sexism, as flaunted in the Arizona professor's letter. And yet admitting just enough of the hidden analogy in order publicly to refute it evokes a further question: if a campus could be compared to a country, what country would it be? Dziech insists in reading Hawaii on the model of another state, "sunny" California (whose mention precedes Hawaii in the professor's letter); she is pleased to say she teaches in Ohio. But what if, as the comparison to a colonized island suggests, there is a national text to the whole issue of sexual harassment?

Let me compare another country, Brazil. During a year there I repeatedly tried to engage a number of Brazilian professors in some sort of discourse about the issue of sexual harassment. There is no such discourse in Brazil. Even the people most conversant with U.S. life seemed to be unaware about how urgent an issue it is in the United States. "If we knew a professor and a student were having sex," one woman said to me, "we would wonder about their feelings—were they happy and so on. We might think they were foolish. But it wouldn't occur to us to censure them." But what about the possibility of the professor exploiting the student? I insisted. The woman smiled, and cited the old saw about there being no sin below the equator. Brazilians, in my experience, like this line, if only because it distinguishes them from sin-soaked North Americans.

Another Brazilian professor told me the following story. During the time she was studying for her master's degree, she happened to mention a certain book to one of her teachers. She needed it for research. He had a copy, and invited her to accompany him to his office where he would get it. When they got there, the professor rummaged around at his desk, until suddenly he reached over and put his arm around the woman's waist. She was shocked, incredulous. Without uttering a word, she got up and left the office.

Not another word was spoken between the woman and the professor during the rest of the semester. She had no further objection either about his behavior or her grade. During the next year—her final one at the campus—the professor spoke to her briefly a couple of times. It seemed to her he wanted to make some sort of statement, or perhaps offer an explanation. But the woman said nothing more to him.

Didn't she think she had been sexually harassed? I asked. She wasn't sure how to reply. "What is sexual harassment?" She said she was afraid of the professor afterwards, lest he try to take further advantage or revenge of some sort. She had to act very carefully in his presence. He had caused her some pain. So there were ways in which she could say she had been sexually harassed. And yet I believe this woman associated harassment with the idea of repetition or duration. In this sense, she had not been so much harassed as exposed to a single instance of a man's sexual desire, and this one instance in itself failed to constitute harassment.

How to explain why a woman could countenance the distinction? I want to suggest two culturally specific explanations. One has to do with the highly overvalued (as it seems to North Americans) and almost desexualized notion of a professor to Brazilians. Professors in Brazil enjoy strong cultural patrimony. Indeed, in contrast, it's tempting to speculate that the power of sexual harassment as an issue in the United States has partly to do with a loss in the social and cultural prestige of professors.[6] Brazilian professors, on the other hand, have suffered no corresponding loss. Behind the professor is the *padrinho,* the godfather whose authority is the very foundation of the social structure.

A second explanation is more interesting still. The woman was most emphatic that she would not have resorted to some sort of legal action. Brazilians do not believe in the law as North Americans do. There are any number of ways to explain the difference. Brazilian law, for example, is less changeable than U.S. law, which is the result of statutes rather than codes. Moreover, Brazilians (like Latin Americans generally) take the law to be less an impersonal system than one expressive of class-based interests. They have no interest in testing the law, but only distrusting it, or, better, avoiding it altogether.

Americans, on the other hand, feel a need to put their faith to the test. The very idea of sexual harassment amounts to a ritual interrogation of the institutional apparatus to see how responsive it remains to social change, or whether the confidence invested in its procedural integrity continues to be justified. The test can be posed more crudely: we need to see if the law remains *virile.* At one point, after lamenting how "the process of formal complaint wears the victim down," Dziech and Weiner sound a hopeful note: "Higher education is not truly impotent in the face of sexual harassment."[7] Precisely. The challenge anything to do with sex poses to academic procedures casts doubt on the potency of these procedures if the issue is not faced, as it were, man-to-man.

Of course to read the national text of sexual harassment is not to approve the fact that some men everywhere feel free to put their arms around the waists of their students, or worse. To each country, we might simply agree, its own ways of dealing with the legal and social constraints upon sexuality in the setting of higher education. A friend told me of the case of a man who got a Fulbright to an African country, came back home to the United States to resign his position after a year, and then returned to Africa to teach there permanently. He had learned that professors in this particular country were expected to have sex with their students. My friend never learned the country's name. Could it be possible to say that sexual harassment there would consist in a professor *withholding* sexual favors? In American terms, the possibility is so bizarre as to be culturally unintelligible.[8]

Yet in terms of many other countries, even ones with traditions closer to our own, the discourse of sexual harassment is only understandable, I think, because it can be associated with a certain kind of peculiarly "American" righteousness, founded on religious principles. These are too familiar to need to be explained. Or rather, they require only to be explained in a certain way. Take the following example, from a president's memo accompanying my university's booklet on sexual harassment: "While it should never be the practice of a university to regulate rather than to stimulate thinking, and while Clarion will always be committed to the free exchange of ideas on any range of topics, certain matters need our critical attention and warrant certain standardized policy statements. Sexual harassment is one of these and the University's statement on sexual harassment is attached for your information."

The routine affirmations of humanistic pieties about the goals of education are absorbed so smoothly into the bland imperatives of the memo style that no one could determine, on the basis of the memo alone, why the "information" is being circulated at all. This is not one of those documents which strives to clarify the conditions of its own production, but instead takes them to be self-explanatory, as if the very subject of sexual harassment simply elicits the need for exceptional regulation and standardization.[9] Only at the conclusion of the booklet does another sort of piety appear. Under a section describing "Sanctions and Remedies," we read the following statement: "The overall remedy desired in sexual harassment cases is the removal of the cause of the complaint and the making whole of the victim."

Represented here, I think, is something of the logic of religious conversion. In terms of such logic, Packard Schmidt agrees to write his letter, above. It might be impossible to see how a victim can be "made whole." It is quite possible to see how a "cause" can be removed—or at least be made to seem so, after being incarnated in one person. "Institutions for which doctrine is central to identity," writes Scott, "are . . . less often concerned with the genuineness of confessions of heresy and recantations than with the public show of unanimity they afford."[10] For a secular society, the university is preeminently one of those institutions.

Mustang Sally makes clear that, in Scott's terms, Packard has written a caricature of a public transcript. But there is something more revealed by the story, and more insidious. Packard (after being "detenured" when the dean finds out about his affair with a colleague's daughter, who works at a brothel) eventually tries to further his career by inviting two prostitutes to serve on his Modern Language Association panel, "The Leukemic Muse of Literary Eroticism: Is Sex Dead or Just Immune-Suppressed?" The results are not entirely happy. Fists as well as slogans fly. But in the process it becomes clear that the "cause" of sexual harassment may be virtually inseparable from the very structure of disciplinary life. How could its biggest annual convention not thrive on surprising convergences with the larger culture, and bold provocations of all sorts, especially including sexual ones? But what then of the pedagogical scene back home, and the relation between what happens at the convention and what happens on campus? We need to see how the discourse of sexual harassment influences the way this relation is currently assumed, if at all, to be understood.

There is an interesting sequence in Joyce Carol Oates's novel, *Marya*, once the heroine of that name becomes "Professor Knauer" at a small, prestigious college in New Hampshire. There she faces two problems. One is tenure. No woman has ever been awarded tenure. The other problem is Sylvester, the lumbering, jeering, middle-aged black custodian. Sylvester leaves Marya's desk drawers slightly open, crushes cigarette butts in her potted plants, and so on. Everyone knows he's "difficult," but he belongs to the union and he can't be fired.

One day Marya tries to confront Sylvester, and he sullenly blunts her. Another day, away from campus, she sees him on the street, all dressed up and walking with a woman. Sylvester doesn't reply when Marya says hello. After this her office window is left open and her desk becomes rain-soaked. Marya doesn't know what to do. She's busy trying to teach well and publish more so she can get tenure.

Her male colleagues urge Marya to shrug Sylvester off. They also refuse to understand when she tells them that they shouldn't be competing against each other because it makes friendship among them impossible. No one learns of the time when, late one day, Marya surprises Sylvester, ostensibly cleaning but in fact seated at her desk. "You black bastard," she mutters.

One spring week, during which rumors are flying about whose contract will be renewed and who will be granted tenure, the chairman calls Marya in to inform her that her contract will be renewed for three years. She returns to her office, and notes that once again the window she has left open has been closed. Then Marya retires to her private lavatory, where she is confronted by the spectacle of a cigarette butt floating in the unflushed toilet.

It seems to me the least interesting question we can ask about this

sequence of events is if Marya is being sexually harassed. She is being harassed, but not sexually. Nothing Sylvester says or does has any overt sexual content. A far more provocative question would be whether Sylvester
considers himself to be harassed by Marya—perhaps, through her aloof-
ness, even sexually.[11] Or should we understand that there is a system within
which each is so impersonally embedded that "harassment," whether or
not of a sexual nature, simply becomes a sort of outwardly melodramatic,
personalized description for the pressure of a structure that neither understands?

The model for this structure is class, not gender. The easiest way to understand Sylvester's actions is as a species of class protest. Marya and her
junior colleagues in the department, in contrast, have no means of protest,
although, by alternating their moments of contact with the custodian's actions, the novel locates them along the same subordinated level of power.
Of course Marya is allotted far more relative power in the institutional hierarchy than Sylvester. Moreover, through her writing, if not her teaching,
she can partake far more directly of the forces that dominate her—and, if
she receives tenure, effectively alter the conditions of her subordination.
Sylvester, although he does have a union, has no such future.

Instead, he can only harass Marya—as a custodian to a faculty member,
as a black man to a white woman, and as a man to a woman. These are
multiple, uneven distinctions. I see no way that Oates's narrative makes
them—to use a word that could get Marya tenure—commensurable with
each other. What the institutional narrative of sexual harassment aims to
do, on the other hand, is to sort such distinctions out by grounding them
in sex, which is exactly the thing that *Marya* fails to clarify or even establish in the first place. In failing to do so, the novel demonstrates something
far more disturbing: the whole academic order—its class hierarchies, its
peculiar insecurities—can be described as harassing in its effect insofar as
sexuality must be emptied out entirely from it.

Therefore to emphasize how harassment can be given the specificity of
a personal, sexual definition is to put back what the conditions of academic life themselves omit. The omission isn't the same at all levels, of course.
The friendship Marya's colleagues spurn among each other is different
than the friendship Marya is structurally excluded from having with the
custodian. The omission is not necessarily experienced consciously. In the
novel, the only exception is perhaps Marya herself, who thereby enacts a

version of the type of the professor characterized by Dziech and Weiner: underpaid and unrewarded, except in narrow professional terms, such as tenure, which tend to count for more to the extent that everything else, such as job mobility, counts for less. *The Lecherous Professor* reads "the professional crisis" in exclusively male terms.[12] *Marya* suggests, on the contrary, that "the crisis" is more elusive, irrespective of gender, and intimate with the whole disposition of institutional power, which dominates everybody and satisfies nobody, neither custodian nor faculty.

It would probably be too facile to claim that sex compensates for this felt subordination—either the sex that actually takes place on campus, or the sex that discursively is not supposed to take place because it constitutes harassment. Similarly, it would undoubtedly be too easy to attribute the rise of sexual harassment as an academic issue during the last decade to any one primary cause—whether the continuing institutionalization of feminism, the aging of the faculty, or some larger failure of politics outside the academy. I would like to explore one more factor because it names, I think, a far more inclusive feature of the issue: narrative. Sexual harassment textualizes the institution's story, and in particular the question of whether each specific one is potent with law or not.

Therefore, embedded within an institution, what narrative authority can more personal stories claim? "Is it true what they're saying about liberal arts education in America?" begins Mark Edmundson in the introduction to his new collection of essays by academics "writing back" against popular misconceptions of American universities.[13] Of course it's not true. The answer that Edmundson and his contributors wish to give is that Western culture is safe, even though there is good reason for it to be questioned from a wide and invigorating range of intellectual perspectives. But what is not quite clear is how this story is related to the fact that, as Edmundson remarks, the essays turn out mostly to be so autobiographical. Could one thing the public is saying about higher education be that its authority now needs to be made good in personal ways because it lacks conviction in larger professional or institutional terms?

If so, nobody among Edmundson's contributors gives such a justification, and I believe the narrative of sexual harassment explains why, while at the same time it prompts the need to tell some autobiographical story in the first place: sexual harassment makes the personal *incompatible* with professional or institutional life. Moreover, sexual harassment re-centers the scene of higher education on the student, and on the nature of the contact between student and teacher. In contrast, none of Edmundson's contributors says much of anything specific about students, and, with one exception (to which I will turn in a moment) nothing at all about sex. The subjects they do talk about, besides themselves, are politics and literary theory. That is, nobody is either autobiographical or pedagogical *enough*, and so, instead, each comprises a specific reason why the public is either telling other stories or having other stories told to it, all of a less transcendent nature.

One thing that distinguishes Jane Gallop's recent essay, "Knot a Love Story," on the other hand, is that she faces the question of writing a personal narrative far more directly, and attempts to integrate private, professional, institutional, and even theoretical dimensions of her life. Her account is unusually compelling because it strives to make inseparable what the narrative of sexual harassment declares to be irreconcilable: the relationship between teaching and sex. How to tell the story of teaching (not to say academic life) without telling the story of sex? Gallop can't—and it's the story she *can't* tell that enthralls her, and perhaps defeats her.

Gallop did not have sex with the student she fell in love with, and she didn't sexually harass him. They never touched. Nothing happened. Yet such was the degree of her "erotic investment" that it would not have been so intense had she not aspired to sex, or had the meetings with the student in her office been entirely free from "harassment" (a word she doesn't use). "The eros was not a deviation, a distraction, an addition, an aside," Gallop writes, "it arose in the center of what was a 'purely pedagogical' exchange, as pure as any such can be."[14] What to conclude? The pedagogical exchange as she presents it seems ultimately to be radically impure, full of hapless role-playing, enticing inequalities of gender and power, and inescapable entanglements of reality and fantasy.

It may even be worse still. Gallop refers to earlier affairs, with women as well as men. In her contribution to Edmundson's collection, Eve Kosofsky Sedgwick concludes as a teacher of gay and lesbian studies with a tribute to the human necessity for more creative expressions of sexuality. She concedes, though, that there appears to be wide popular resentment against college faculty because such possibilities are "to a degree, built into the structure of our regular paid labor." It seems to Sedgwick that there is nothing to be done about sexuality but to enjoy it, flamboyantly, as one can. "Sexuality in this sense, perhaps," she continues, "can *only* mean queer sexuality. So many of us have the need for spaces of thought and work where everything doesn't mean the same thing!"[15]

Must the classroom, then, be one of these spaces? How many energies is the classroom still culturally imperiled to conserve rather than release in American society today? Of course it cannot be determined how directly the discourse of sexual harassment addresses the entrance of homosexuality into contemporary representations of sexuality. However, it is easy to see how the discourse, which became visible at more or less the same time, is challenged by homosexuality. "Queerness" profoundly unsettles the familiar gender assignments of victimizer and victim in the harassment scenario, as well as the kinds of erotic investments customarily made in the pedagogical exchange according to the model of heterosexual desire.[16]

It seems to me that an additional burden on the discourse of sexual harassment is to shore up the sort of popular resentment against college professors Sedgwick mentions, especially as it pertains both to class and to "queer" sexuality. Furthermore, the same discourse functions at least to stabilize the resentment within the boundaries of a heterosexual narrative. Such an agenda need not be explicitly set out. Public transcripts do not have to justify themselves in this way. All that is required is that erotic investments be specified. Many sorts of different narratives will be purged into the bargain.

&

Let me cite the list of offenses from my university's booklet on sexual harassment:

> Specific examples of sexual harassment would include, but are not limited to: sexually suggestive gestures, comments, innuendos, jokes, or questions of a sexual nature; remarks that stigmatize or ridicule others on the basis of gender or affectional preference; inappropriate use of sexually oriented materials; unwanted letters, phone calls, or interviews which discuss personal sexual matters; unwanted cornering or leaning over; inappropriate or unwanted touching, pinching, or patting; pressure for sexual favors; and attempted or actual sexual assault or rape.

From within the context of Gallop's discourse, several of these items read like lost narrative possibilities—some lost in her own narrative (it being inconceivable that the "exchange" she describes was entirely free of innuendo or physically "proximal" indiscretion), some perhaps unrepresentable in any. These latter sorts of possibilities are apparently those solicited by Sedgwick, legality and literality be damned.

Perhaps there must always be something unrepresentable in a sexual narrative. This is why Gallop finally locates her story somewhere indeterminately between a knowledge that can be publicly shared and a fiction that need be accountable only to itself. In contrast, the above list is confident of its status as knowledge, and simply has no status if it is not applicable to everyone. It does not tell a story but instead mandates a policy. Stories are too vividly individual, too waywardly circumstantial, and never fit into policies very well. Furthermore, in stories a public text turns out to be strangely subversive, a social relation is all knotted up with sexual force, and sex does not necessarily appear in terms of power.

It may well be that the narrative of human relations in academic life today, whether told with crudity or sophistication, can only be given accurately in terms of what it is not, because the sexual "knot" has been severed. The enormous power of the discourse of sexual harassment to issue its own "warrant" has resulted in unprecedented institutional recognition and statutory constraint. It feels like writing fiction for me to add, with respect to my own institution, that the above phrase, "affectional preference," had to be removed, according to the president's memo, on the advice of legal counsel.

Such constraint, however, operates at the price of a profound irony. It turns out that personal life can be mandated as incompatible with professional or institutional life because in fact both the opportunity and the provocation of sex—and therefore of harassment—is all too compatible. Margaret Talbot begins her account of the Jane Gallop harassment case with the following perspective on Gallop's teaching style: "Close relationships between advisers and advisees may be rife with difficulties, but they are the best initiation into the academic life that anyone has yet devised."[17] Precisely. It is as much in the interests of any university to keep relationships between advisers and advisees indeterminate as it is to preserve the very role of adviser.

If as a result of this indeterminateness sexual exploitation may occur as a consequence, it is more than offset by the gain in organizational efficiency, not to say clarification. Indeed, imagining a university without advisers proves to be as impossible as imagining one without hierarchy. Another recent book on campus sexual harassment begins a chapter with the following elementary point about "power and status inequities ripe for exploitation": "Academic institutions are structured hierarchically."[18] How to banish the presence of "categorical rank" from university president down through faculty and students, and even including custodial staff? Once more, it appears to be as impossible as banishing an "inequity" in knowledge between teacher and student internal to the pedagogical scene itself.

At one point, according to Talbot's account, Gallop's two accusers orchestrated a demonstration against her during a local conference in which Day-Glo bumper stickers were sold that read "Distinguished Professors Do It Pedagogically." How to respond? Distinction, of course, is another of the things internal to the whole project of education; indeed, the more prominent of the two accusers came to the University of Wisconsin at Milwaukee for the express purpose of studying under Gallop. What distinguished professors such as she illustrate is the same thing less distinguished ones do: to do it at all pedagogically is to risk doing it sexually— and therefore to risk harassment according to someone's definition.

One of Roiphe's prototypical feminists, Sarah, once tells her of a fantasy-ideal university, which would be free of hierarchy (as well as grades, syllabi, competition, and sexism). Sarah disagrees when Roiphe objects that her ideal only creates a new hierarchy based on the restored value of oppressed groups.[19] An additional objection could well be made: the ideal is based on the purgation of sexuality itself. As Roiphe's own initial chapter makes clear, freshpersons of the 1990s are initiated into a vision of college life including condoms, rape counselors, and the threat of AIDS. The climate could not be further from that of a progressive liberal arts college of the 1940s, where in her once-famous fictional recreation, *The Groves of Academe*, Mary McCarthy's knowing narrator could write in the following way of a professor greeting a student in his office and contemplating whether to tell her a shocking item of personal news: "He felt himself gliding, by rhythmic easy stages, into the girl's confidence; the knowledge that there, in the file, lay that which would disrupt her faith in officialdom gave him a sense of power over her and all her virgin classmates. . . . now a slight shifting of the girl's weight in her chair made him imagine that he had lost his hold on her."[20]

McCarthy's professor might not be harassing the student in deed. Yet one can only read the description today in amazement. It must be conceded that he is harassing her in thought. A vision of sexuality based on dominance, struggle, and control is too much with us now. The campus, even in its most casual, innocent occasions, is irretrievably sexualized. Even critics of harassment codes admit: "People can have orgasms sitting in class listening to a good lecture."[21] Sex is going to mediate the relations of even the most caring professors (as McCarthy's Henry Mulcahy is presented to be) or else they will have to give up caring. One assumes, however, that they will not be asked to stay away from their offices, or strive not to give good lectures.

It might as well be admitted: a university aiming to rule out the possibility of sexual harassment (and not simply legislate against it) is going to have to put even the privacies of sexual fantasy to shame, along with the dominant public conditions that foster such fantasies. The only way to prevent such action is for individuals to counter with better stories about universities in which the most private, unrepresentable moments among teachers and students are shown to be utterly compatible with academic life. Not only because, if it were not so, academic life finally would not be life. If its initiations and abuses were not all of a piece, academic life would not even be academic.

Chapter Two

Personal Authority,
Colonial Power, and
Dissertation Directors

No significant figure in American higher education is more conspicuously absent in its discourse than that of the dissertation director. To write a dissertation you have to have a director (a term I'll try to use to include that of "adviser"). It appears to be equally a fact that public recognition of his or her presence in the whole project of producing a dissertation must be either consigned to a grateful line or two in the acknowledgments (if a candidate is lucky enough to get the dissertation published) or else abandoned to the more private anecdotal realm.

Of course one reason nothing is mentioned about dissertation directors is because nothing is mentioned about the actual writing of dissertations. Paul Cantor justly begins his contribution to a recent publication of the Modern Language Association, *The Future of Doctoral Studies in English*, by referring to "the forgotten part of the graduate curriculum: the dissertation years." "The typical graduate student in English," he continues, "spends at least as many years working on the dissertation as he or she does taking classes."[1] But then Cantor goes on to consider these years not in terms of this work, but instead with respect to the job market.

At least "the dissertation years" have some specificity in Cantor's account.

To the rest of the contributors in the volume, these years have none. Everyone else is concerned about course work: should there be more Aristotle and less Derrida, or more rhetoric and less literature? In addition, much ink is spilled over the need for general requirements and special colloquia. The desiderata of improved teaching is honored, and, in the last section, attention is even paid to how much teaching graduate students themselves have to do.

The dissertation years, however, are left, like those who write dissertations, to fend for themselves. From the point of view of any one institution's program, what this means in practice, I think, is that these years become more or less the sole official responsibility of one individual: the dissertation director. It is the director who works with a candidate on the initial stages of a dissertation proposal, and then supervises its articulation over as many chapters and drafts as he or she deems need to be done, for however many years it takes. The director can be presumed to do everything over the course of a candidate's writing from providing continual encouragement and suggesting new bibliography to giving mini-grammar lessons and pouring the coffee.

It is hard to direct a dissertation. Each one, like each person who writes one, has its special demands—nuances that take weeks to get right, critical perspectives that should have been more evident sooner, and so on. In the following account, I am going to write from the position of the candidate rather than the director, because it is the candidate who more powerfully represents the space of the subordinated, from which, as usual, an impeccably public transcript has to emerge.[2] Of course I do not mean to gainsay how many directors prove to be just as decent, patient, and crucial as acknowledgments say they have been. My discussion is about representation, not accuracy; or rather, about the hidden silence in the construction of dominant representation.

A recent article in *Lingua Franca* on the increase of completion times for the doctorate (the median duration is now over twelve years in the humanities) focuses on a new grant program by the Mellon Foundation aimed at reducing the time, but finds that this program, like an earlier one sponsored by the Ford Foundation, slights the role that the dissertation itself plays in any doctoral program: "Rethinking the nature of dissertations was and still is politically unwise because it challenges the authority of the faculty who direct these projects, and faculty support is crucial to any effort to shorten completion times."[3] What I want to discuss is not so much why re-thinking dissertations has been deemed unwise but why representing dissertation directors is virtually unthinkable.

ɞ

If we consider how dissertations are produced in the rest of the world, I think we see more bluntly their most fundamental circumstances, even in the United States: one individual, alone, writes under the authority of one other individual, the director. No one else is involved. These two are solely responsible for working out their schedule of meetings or writing deadlines. There are no doctoral programs in Brazil, for example, that provide any other provision for "the dissertation years." Compared to the United States, Brazil is instructive because it has very few institutions that can grant a Ph.D., and therefore, as in so many other countries, the master's degree is the more typical one among faculty, with the thesis often acquiring the significance of a dissertation. Consequently, for faculty who have managed to complete enough course work to advance to the dissertation stage, it is common for Brazilian universities to grant special paid leaves up to four years. I met a woman who had one for two years. She had failed to write a word in a year and a half. She had not taken another job, as many chronically underpaid Brazilian teachers do, even though they are prohibited by the conditions of their leave. Instead, she had taken an overnight bus a number of times to consult with her director, some five hundred kilometers away. The man summarily rejected everything she tried to write, and gave her absolutely no help at all on how to proceed, much less about how to conceive of a coherent subject.

Of course one does not have to travel to Brazil to hear such stories. Indeed, in my experience they're so common that one can only wonder anew, each time, how a dissertation ever gets written anywhere. The complaint is always the same: directors don't care. They might get released time to direct dissertations or they might not. The number of dissertations produced may give a program more university-wide clout or it may not. In any case, even people who have completed dissertations often bemoan how there is simply no way to make a dissertation director responsible, no department-wide body to which his or her inattentions (or worse) might be accountable.

It might be said that responsible directors are all alike, but each irresponsible director is irresponsible in his or her own way. The most interesting dissertation director stories often confound the very difference, if not some stable notion of responsibility. Take one of an American woman who was told, after her director agreed to work with her (the program being so small he had little choice), to go away and not come back until she had written an entire draft. Fine, the woman felt. She knew enough about her habits of composition to feel that she would not have benefited from chapter-by-chapter supervision anyway.[4] Her draft, with cursory revisions, made it past the languid eye of the director in less than a year.

Meanwhile her best friend, who reached dissertation stage around the same time, remained blocked. Another year passed before he began his own dissertation, under the direction of the same man, whose protégé he was. This man received far more of the director's care, if not exactly the chapter-by-chapter sort. Hence, her friend was the more astonished when, during the latter stages of his writing, the director sent him a book and an article that had in fact to do with the subject of the woman's dissertation, completed, by this time, almost two years before.

"Interesting," he opined to the director, who then asked if the man had incorporated it into his last chapter. "What do you mean? I just thought you meant the stuff as general reading. Don't you remember the subject of my dissertation?" Alas, it turned out, the director really did not. He had confused one candidate for the other, even though years separated them and their respective subjects had little in common. If the director had been more conventionally responsible to his protégé, it turned out that he was apparently no less idle.

Though for some candidates how much a director awakens to a project might spell the difference between completing and not completing a dissertation, who can say how often responsible action just misses being irresponsible, and is not even classifiable as a difference in kind? When I heard the above story I was immediately reminded of a friend embarrassed to talk about how quickly he wrote his dissertation. Once he admitted why. His director had taken a job at a more prestigious university and was so enthralled at the big career move of his life that he really didn't care much what my friend wrote. So it only took a semester to complete. Moreover, one reason the committee subsequently approved the dissertation so easily, my friend now surmises, is that everybody was anxious not to offend their ascendant colleague. He might matter for their own futures. One never knows.

And yet no one never reads. Stories such as this are important to record, like stories about the actual circumstances of sexual harassment. The public record of how dissertations actually get written, much less accepted, comprehends little of the highly personal, makeshift, and frequently arbitrary nature of the conditions. A collection of autobiographical accounts on the writing of dissertations, including some on directing them, would mark, I think, a significant moment at least in the inner life of American higher education. As it is, however, I believe we must characterize some larger public understanding of this life as being either too mundane, or just too muffled.[5]

Too bad. The "dissertation years" are usually full of suspense and outward significance. My sense is that no period of a career, not even the year or two before a tenure decision, can be more fraught with drama, agony, despair, provocation, and elation—sometimes all at once, unbearably. Moreover, the "symbolic capital" of a Ph.D. guarantees the very possibility of a career like no other academic award.[6] Was this the reason a man I once vaguely knew went clinically mad while trying to write a dissertation? He never quite made contact with his director, who can be forgiven, I suppose, for never quite knowing what to do with someone who kept thrusting chapters at him like weapons.

The peculiar plot involved in writing a dissertation can be comprehended in the following way: in no phase of an academic life is one individual more thoroughly under the power of another. Some cannot tolerate it. The consequences of subordination, for better or worse, reverberate throughout the rest of a career, beginning with the discursive (if not more narrowly political) conditions mandating how the candidate's relation with the director is represented. I have already suggested that the power of the director must be recreated by the candidate as benign authority. In particular, whether or not the relation has come to grief, this power must not be presented in terms of the director having indulged in individual whims.

Such whims, in turn, are the essence of the essential complaint anyone has about a director during the course of writing a dissertation—for instance, getting initially, and then repeatedly, dismissed from the office door, and having no recourse but to return. The power of the whimsical matters. The whimsical *is* power. Dissertation directors can afford to be "busy," as well as just busy. Candidates can afford to be neither. "Power means *not having to act*," James Scott emphasizes, "or, more accurately, the capacity to be more negligent and casual about any single performance."[7] Whims represent the most important single feature about the nature of director's peculiar authority: its absolute nature.

If we ask why it is absolute, the answer seems to be simple: it is personal. Why the authority of a dissertation director is personal, however, is not at all easy to explain, especially when set against a background where virtually every other aspect of an academic's professorial behavior — from how to address a dean to what to write on the requisite syllabus distributed the first day of a course — can be so exquisitely rationalized, routinized, and codified. At this point I want to relate another, more complicated story about the writing of a dissertation. The university was Yale. To name the director in question, one of the literary profession's more distinguished names, would be to risk libel. I mention the danger because absolute power always makes what can be said about it partial. There are limits, after all, to what can be written about the figure of a dissertation director, and perhaps the most one can do is mark the limits.

The particular candidate, a woman, went to the man with her proposal carefully written out. She chose him because of his eminence. She had heard nothing about him personally. The man glanced at the proposal, and told her to rewrite it. She was afraid to object that he had hardly read her pages. So she rewrote them, took the proposal back to the man, and once again watched his casual dismissal.

This time the woman objected. "How can you say that? Don't you know how important my dissertation is to me?" "Look," the eminence replied, "we can do this in an afternoon. It won't be hard. There's nothing about this proposal that should cause you any difficulty at all." Then he paused. The woman swore she didn't expect what was coming next. "All you have to do is sleep with me. Just once."

She snapped up her proposal and left the office immediately. What to do next? She did not want to tell even her husband. She did not. A few days passed. Finally she decided to go to the graduate director and state that she wanted another adviser. But when she did so, things were not quite so simple: the program had a rule that a student could only change advisers once, and a change could only be approved if reasons were given in writing and signed by the adviser.

One year passed before the woman could bring herself to go back to the man. Then she asked him, flatly, to sign a statement she would write, to the unexceptionable effect that the two of them just could not agree about the "precise direction" of her project. "I'll do it," he said. "But if I do you'll regret it." He did it. She regretted it.

The now-former adviser enjoyed enough power in the department to be able successfully to maneuver one of his protégés, a new assistant professor, onto the woman's dissertation committee. This man proceeded to object to everything she brought before the committee: chapters always needed much more work, the project still lacked clarity, and so on. Eventually it took four years for the woman to write her dissertation. When it was finally approved, the protégé agreed to sign off, he publicly declared, out of sympathy only, for in his opinion the dissertation still was not worth much.

What to conclude? I believe that to categorize such an experience solely as an example of sexual harassment slights the full horror of the experience. Granted, sex is central to the story. But the peculiar harassment the woman's experience is about is not finally sexual.[8] I am not sure it has a name. Or that it has to. The most striking thing about the story, to me, is that it concerns three texts by the same author: a proposal, a letter, and a dissertation. Each one of them is embedded in an increasingly intricate network of private motives that acts to disable the author from having some final authority over her words. In this sense, the harassment is textual rather than sexual.

In another sense, the harassment—but now the word is too immediate and blunt—has to do with what defines discursive authority. It is possible of course to give the circumstances a kind of analysis that one invariably associates with Michel Foucault. The relations of power don't merely consist of domination and subjection. Power is institutional, disciplinary, diffuse, impersonal, and so on.[9] However, the striking fact about the authority of the dissertation director is that it is *not* any of these things. It is personal. *Who* the particular director is matters enormously. Nothing about how any director at once embodies and relays larger displacements of power would have operated as it did in the above case if the woman had gone to someone else.

Indeed, the dissertation director's authority is so strikingly different from the Foucauldian model as to make one wonder whether the academic popularity of Foucault in recent decades has not functioned as a kind of willed forgetting that power as a discursive practice needs to be activated by specific people, as well as located in them. How thoroughly true this is of academic life itself may be a matter of dispute. What is not disputable is that any profession is traversed by structures of authority emanating from the most private motives and spread through personal contacts and local lines of influence. The dissertation director effectively initiates his or her charge into these structures.[10] The woman in the above story went to her Yale man because she didn't want someone who would lack the capacity to do so by not having enough influence.

What she didn't know was the price of success: a compliance so total that her opposition to it could not be represented—not in her proposal, not in her letter, and not in her dissertation itself. Each successive text is an example of what James Scott has termed a public transcript. The important thing about these transcripts is that they constitute a writing of the dominant: "The capacity of dominant groups to prevail—though never totally—in defining and constituting what counts as the public transcript and what as offstage is . . . no small measure of their authority."[11] I would only add in the above case that the dominant group prevailed because of the insistent motives of one powerful man.

Of course it could also be emphasized that the dominant group prevailed because through it a dissertation was once again enforced as strictly public theater. No offstage allowed. In its pages no one attacks one's director, much less a former one, because the script allows only for an expression of indebtedness. Nevertheless, in this context Scott's reading of discursive authority is to be preferred to Foucault's, I believe, because the precise "form of domination" represented by the dissertation director commands subjugated figures whose "family resemblance" is to the slaves, serfs, colonized and otherwise dominated races of Scott's account. Each of these groups suffers because there is virtually nothing any of them can do about it, and, more to my point, nothing they can write about it that won't have to be, in his sense, "hidden."[12]

About the precise kinds of domination in such circumstances, Scott explains as follows: "They embody formal assumptions about superiority and inferiority, often in elaborate ideological form, and a fair degree of ritual and 'etiquette' regulates public conduct within them." "Although highly institutionalized," he continues, "these forms of domination typically contain a strong element of personal rule." Scott specifically mentions that the rule is "infused by an element of personal terror that may take the form of arbitrary beatings, sexual violations, and other insults and humiliations. Whether or not they occur to any particular subordinate, the ever-present knowledge that they might seems to color the relationship as a whole."[13]

In the case above, the adviser's declaration of his sexual intent constitutes the "infusion" of sexual violation. Moreover, his later statement to the woman that she would regret her departure from his authority promised the public humiliation that he was confident he could initiate—as, through his protégé, he eventually did. It would not be accurate on the basis of such an example to claim that a dissertation director can get away with anything. Many graduate programs (and I have deliberately omitted consideration of small ones) can undoubtedly point to committees designed, in part, to monitor abuse. The trouble is, in the above story the committee comprises part of the abuse. For better and worse, a director can get away with just about anything.

At the heart of any doctoral institution's thicket of structures lies a "subsystem" of one, the figure of the dissertation director, who constitutes the most prominent vanishing point of an individual figure in the organization of higher education. There is too much in any one relation with a candidate that simply cannot be monitored, and even instances of a director acting out of more proper, professional motives reveal how unrepresentable, and perhaps even incommunicable, the exercise of a director's personal power proves to be.

How to assess it? How to assess personal power generally in the academy? I believe the need lies behind a recent spate of books designed not only to open up the programs of individual disciplines to wider public scrutiny, but to set out for prospective academics the more practical exigencies of professional life. It is now possible for the graduate student or the young professor to consult volumes about the best time frame in which to publish a second book or the most "collegial" ways to get along with colleagues. This last consideration, in fact, is the subject of a contribution in a recent collection of essays, *The Art and Politics of College Teaching*. A section on ethics poses for the junior faculty member a problem about no less a figure than a dissertation director. The case ("drawn from actual experience") provides an instructive fictional counterpart to the true story I outlined above. Once again, the peculiarity about a dissertation director has to do with what cannot be said.

A senior professor is given as having overstepped the boundaries in guiding his charge through all stages of the dissertation process. He has written all the questions for her comprehensive examination, and then, contrary to "accepted policy," graded them. A committee, in deferring judgment on the professor, actually promises approval if the man gets the student—long regarded around the department as a general nuisance—graduated as soon as possible. He proceeds to do most of the actual writing of the woman's dissertation, and to answer all the questions for her on her orals. All members of the committee sign off, and the woman is awarded a Ph.D.

In a sense, this case is the reverse of a narrative of abuse. If the director here can be judged to have been, as the author of the fictional case explains, "too paternalistic," at least it could be argued that he has "acted rightly in putting this human concern before academic concerns."[14] Of course, this could also be a description of what the Yale man did, above, notwithstanding the fact that some human concerns, presumably, accord better to the spirit of a doctoral degree than others. The author of the case is careful not to characterize any sort of self-interest on the part of his man, and instead goes on to worry about the doctoral committee's complicity and most especially a junior faculty member's responsibility as one who is not directly involved but "aware" of the whole situation.

The issues are indeed vexing. What is especially curious, however, in the case as given, is how the director gets lost in them. The graduate student is characterized by a specificity not granted to the dissertation director. As if to make the director more sympathetic, the candidate is given impeccable race, gender, class, and even age credentials: black, female, "from a third-world country," and fifty. The only noteworthy thing about the professor, in contrast, is that he is senior. A novelist would have to flesh him out more—although the temptation might not seem to be very provocative; just so, a critic contemplating an article on "The Image of the Dissertation Director in Modern Fiction" faces a dearth of material.

It is as if the power of the director lies in being not so much unrepresented as unrepresentable. His actions set the terms for the dissertation narrative. But no public transcript can express them except in formulaic terms. Finally, this may be just as much because of the contradictions of academic life as the nature of public transcripts. The figure of the dissertation director is mandated by the institutional system to bear more symbolic freight than most other individuals. Embedded in isolation within an intricate fabric of committees, the director occupies the intersection of two separate, but related, organizations of professional knowledge: one is collaborative, the other hierarchical.

To the extent that knowledge is collaborative, it depends upon social factors: who to get to write a recommendation for you, how to get help with a paper, the right person who knows about a certain category of scholarship, and so on. A dissertation director is perhaps the one formally conceded, structurally embedded example of the phenomenon of "mentoring" in academic life.[15] But the fact that it is necessary to have a director in order to write a dissertation at all does not stipulate how a candidate goes about finding one, much less exactly what a director's duties might be. In a sense, these duties are left as indeterminate as the nature of the social relation itself.

In another sense, though, the duties are indeterminate because the figure of the director absorbs the degraded status of actually writing a dissertation in the first place, as well as the incomplete rationale for its technique (to recall Benjamin). Whether or not this status reflects, in turn, the possibly dubious value of a Ph.D. for every teacher in all fields in order to enjoy the full measure of a career in higher education in the United States is a question of a different sort. The director abides as the voice authorized to give a practical answer to the candidate: you will need help in order to write a dissertation, and I will give it to you.

And yet to the extent that knowledge is hierarchical, even the social relation between candidate and director is expected to be shaped by the discipline. It could be argued that intellectual endeavor in an academic framework must be collaborative because professional knowledge is finally hierarchical: not only must authorities be cited, but the right ones, or the latest ones. Who says which ones count more than others? A dominant class, which it is the burden of the dissertation director to personify. Again, it may be an arguable question whether subordination must be as absolute a fact as I have envisioned it. My point is that the subordination of candidate to director must *risk* being so absolute, each time, because the fact of hierarchy itself is so imperative to learn.

In this sense, of course, the function of a dissertation director changes from the fluid, informal one of mentoring to the more regulated, professionalized one of initiating. "Do we retain the characteristic taste of our class background," the editors of a new collection of essays on working-class women ask, "or does the initiation process of the doctorate dissatisfy us with our backgrounds, instilling in us a desire for elite values and prejudices?"[16] The answer of their contributors is clear: elite values are what academic life is all about. Some jobs are better than others, some institutions are more celebrated than others—and some directors know more influential people than others. In terms of academic hierarchy, writing a dissertation is more about entering a network than rewriting a chapter.

How are these two separate organizations of knowledge related? The answer is much simpler than the question. They are related the only way they could possibly be: on a personal basis. Some individuals are so institutionally favored to affect the relation between collaborative and hierarchical that collaboration probably seems like another version of hierarchy, or vice versa. But, as the example from Yale above makes clear, this does not mean that such people will be able to give either practical or professional help to anyone when asked. Indeed, the personal basis of the disposition of knowledge in the academy guarantees nothing. Instead, we see this basis repeatedly effaced as if it were an embarrassment. And yet personal dynamics will not go away, especially not in order to produce the inaugural public transcript of an academic career.

The figure of the dissertation director marks the one space where the personal in academic life is officially allowed to operate fully, albeit only in the service of something else—a dissertation. I have tried to make clear that in fact this space continues to be useful to the politics of academic life because so many purposes that meet in the dissertation project are simply irreconcilable, and must therefore be left to work themselves out individually, if at all. There appears to be no other way to formalize the beginning of an academic career than to place a candidate in a position of subordination so complete that the domination cannot be resisted, not even by a hidden transcript.

Of course this does not mean that a candidate is completely without freedom, even at the outset. It does mean that candidates who are going to ponder the meaning of the project are imperiled to do so long after the fact, and not without a certain discretion. Nancy Miller has a recent essay on the evolution of feminist theory in her life in which the writing of her dissertation plays an oblique role. "Despite the hierarchies and abuses of academic conventions," she states, "I saw writing a dissertation as something radical but also literary: as becoming the heroine of my life."[17] However, not only does she disclose that her dissertation was written according to the structuralist imperatives of the time but that her director, "who took the conventions of patriarchy very seriously," was shocked when she decided to change her name.

Miller is not of course obligated to ponder how patriarchy, not to say her director, might have constrained her felt freedom. That she mentions her dissertation director at all is unusual. Yet the fact that she says so little seems to me another instance of how the figure of the dissertation director is an almost wholly absent one, as well as a completely untheorized one, in the discursive practices of American higher education. And meanwhile, the practices of other countries have scarcely begun to take patriarchy into account.

I return to the woman in Brazil who hadn't a clue about writing a dissertation. When I met her, the sole object of her analysis consisted of one text: Somerset Maugham's short story, "The Outstation." I was incredulous. Any American professor would be. She took an hour explaining to me how she wanted to perform some sort of linguistic analysis of the text, according to the theories of one Michel Pecheux, a favorite of the man the woman had chosen as her director. She had a seminar with him.

"The Outstation" is a story about a power struggle between an old British colonial administrator in Borneo, Warburton, and his new assistant, Cooper. Warburton luxuriates in his tenuous personal associations with the aristocracy and dotes on every mention of a peer in the *Times*, which he gets six weeks late. Cooper is full of class resentment. To Cooper, Warburton is an unregenerate snob. To Warburton, Cooper is an unmannered fool.

Relations between the two collapse after Warburton returns from a trip to find Cooper unapologetic at having read his precious *Times* and mixed up the sequence of copies. A letter Warburton writes about Cooper to his superior is rebuked. Eventually Cooper is murdered by one of his servants, whom, despite Warburton's warning about local customs, he has dismissed without his wages, then hit in the face. The story ends with Warburton, content, unfolding one of his copies of the *Times*.

It has long been a fancy of mine that every dissertation is an autobiographical act, especially the longer one waits to write it. The Brazilian woman was in her mid-forties when I met her. She had little to learn about domination and subordination. So did she associate herself with Cooper? I was never able to discuss the story with her. Why did she choose it? She'd been teaching at a provincial state university as long as Warburton had been at his outstation. Perhaps, rather than identify him with her director, she identified with Warburton herself.

This last possibility intrigues me most because Warburton, like her, tries to write something. But we do not read it in the story. "The Outstation" prints only the reply from his superior, which therefore assumes the character of a public transcript reinstituting domination and enforcing hierarchy. Any response Warburton could have attempted would have only functioned as, in Scott's sense, "hidden" and without consequence. The only text the character actually has at his disposal is the *Times*, which of course assumes the guise of a far more public, sovereign writing of the whole system of imperial rule that comprehends nothing so private and inward as the challenge Cooper presents to it. Significantly, I think, Cooper is given no text at all.

I never learned why the Brazilian woman was trying to write a dissertation. Just to get promoted and make more money? And even if it is understandable why someone might dream of writing a dissertation who has taught for so long that she ought more justly to be directing one, what about a person who lacks the benefit of a graduate career, much less a system of higher education, in which a sequence of "the dissertation years" can at least be enunciated? Or is it possible that even with the benefit of a career in such a system, a person can still get very badly mixed up, confusing authority with revolt, or what has to be officially represented with what has to remain hidden?

Of course the totality of one woman's confusion cannot be made to stand for everyone else's. Furthermore, one narrative cannot be made to allegorize the entire problematic of writing a dissertation, especially from an impossibly global perspective. Nonetheless, so much is unknown about the actual process of writing a dissertation—conference by conference, chapter by chapter, month by month—that what *is* known can appear to be virtually nothing when we at least try to include failure into the equation. As it is, the story of success is the only story we have. It seems to me that if we are going to open up the plot lines we can do worse than use a colonial model as a point of entry into our own institutional structures.

David Bromwich has strikingly asserted that academics under siege from both conservatives and liberals decrying standards might now well claim the analogy of academic culture to "a native culture under threat from a colonial power" attempting to preserve its integrity. "The perspective of colonial victims could be, if not the light at the end of the tunnel, certainly an apt and acceptable light in the tunnel itself."[18] He cautions that only someone could employ the argument who is innocent of irony, as presumably he himself is not. Bromwich does not pause to consider, though, the particular irony that the native culture is founded upon colonial power.

Of course a dissertation director—ideally—makes it possible for a candidate to enter the system, either through a post in the provinces or one in the capital. But, although one estimable text is produced as a result of two people having met, another text is suppressed. How does the candidate acquire the necessary authority to write the dissertation within a most specific dynamic of dominance and submission? A completed dissertation testifies solely to the fact of the dynamics having been enacted, but not the authority having necessarily been possessed, much less resisted. Meanwhile, the *Times* merely prints the names of the aristocracy. It is crucial for the director to know these names, and to counsel the candidate on the importance of citing them. For better and worse, we must trust that the candidate learns what the experienced director already knows: the profound difference between those destined for the administrative system and temporary native laborers, who merely like to be well treated.

Chapter Three
Wheels, Cogs, Oil Cups,
and Rejection Letters

When an editor says they are not interested
in your work at the present time they mean
forget about it.

— Gilbert Sorrentino, *Mulligan Stew*

A while ago an envelope appeared in my mailbox, addressed to me in my own hand, on which was stamped the following:

> Opened in the Dead Letter Office
> New York, NY 10199-9543
> Contained No Return Address
> Forwarded: Postage Due.

Inside was a manuscript I had completely forgotten about, submitted perhaps a year or so before, along with the requisite self-addressed, stamped envelope. You always have to include this envelope. It represents how the moment of rejection is built into the action of submitting anything to be published.

The form letter inside my envelope read as follows:

> Thank you for the opportunity to read and consider your work. We are sorry to report that after careful consideration, we have decided against publishing your contributions in our magazine.
>
> The Editors

What had happened? How had my manuscript found its way to the Dead Letter Office? Had the editors made off with my stamps? You simply never know what's going to happen to a piece of unsolicited writing after you submit it. Furthermore, even after it is rejected and returned to you, you never learn exactly why it was rejected.

That is, rejection forms never tell you. These forms, which are standardized, must be distinguished from rejection letters, which are in some way personal or at least personalized. However, this distinction won't hold in actual practice, and many rejection forms are interesting because they reveal the slippage. The mark of the personal on a depersonalized document discloses the whole text of rejection as a strange kind of writing, at once public and private, compromised either way.

Suppose we begin by inquiring why there are rejection forms at all. We could be content to accept that the whole logic of rejection resembles an old joke about the man who goes to a psychiatrist because he thinks there is something wrong with him. "You're crazy," the psychiatrist concludes. The man protests: "Can I get a second opinion?" "All right," says the psychiatrist, "you're ugly, too." It's the burden of rejection forms to enact the same sort of opinion, only much more agreeably and courteously.

Of course some magazines do it better than others. There are all sorts of subtle differences among rejection forms, including ones stating that the magazine, regrettably, has far more hopeful contributors than actual readers or ones that apologize for having to be forms. Nonetheless, rare is the contributor who can expect a rejection such as the following one Thoreau once received from Margaret Fuller after his submission to the *Dial* early in his career: "Last night's second reading only confirms my impression from the first. The essay is rich in thoughts, and I should be pained not to meet it again. But then, the thoughts seem to me so out of their natural order, that I cannot read it through without pain. I never once felt myself in a stream of thought, but seem to hear the grating tools on the mosaic."[1]

Indeed, today such a comment may be rarer than a letter of acceptance. In the same issue of the *New Republic* that I read this quotation, the poetry editor, Mary Jo Salter, has a column mentioning a black trash bag she stuffs with hundreds of unsigned rejection slips, along with a few dozen personal letters of rejection, and takes to her local post office once or twice a month. Why are there rejection forms? Because there are so many potential contributors who must be rejected by so many editors such as Salter. The matter finally seems as simple as that.

It is not. One reason is cultural. Unsolicited material in most nations of the world is not dealt with in terms of rejection forms. Either the material is ignored, and the hopeful contributor receives no reply at all, or else the reply is personal.[2] Rejection forms in the United States are written according to a cultural script. Americans apply for a loan, a job, a grant. Alas, when we are rejected it is most commonly by a standardized form, on which even the signature is presigned, if the form is a letter. American life countenances great impersonality.[3]

Therefore another reason sheer quantity of solicitation alone fails to explain rejection forms is more difficult to examine: the forms are seldom actually without a personal inscription of some sort. Does this mean, in turn, that they assume, or mean to assume, the character of a personal communication? What exactly is the status of the personal in rejection forms? Is the writing meant to be read or just acknowledged? If read, what about the possibility of a reply? Or if merely acknowledged, what sort of a community is being presumed by the form?

It is probably easiest to locate the notion of a community in an academic context. Whether in terms of exalted ideals of scholarship or realistic goals of tenure and professional advancement, those who are rejected and those who reject are likely to share the same interests concerning publication, to have studied the same conventions, and even to occupy both positions, of rejected and rejecter, simultaneously. Moreover, the role of the reader's report broadens the whole base of scholarly activity, and appears to make the site of rejection both more democratic and more just.

However, the realization of community, even in a circumscribed academic space, is an elusive one. David Bromwich calls attention to how ritualistically academics invoke the ideal of community, as a means of compensation for its lack outside the university. "The mission of the university of this view," Bromwich writes, "is to make up the difference between true public need and the poor satisfaction of that need in civil life."[4] Bromwich's point is that it takes more than a word to make up the difference. My plainer point is that it takes more than a rejection letter. An academic finds it no easier to be rejected than anybody else.

Indeed, it seems to me that an academic is finally only a special instance of how an individual contributor's understanding is confounded upon rejection, each time, by a more embracing ignorance. Rejection is experienced very privately. It is not meant to be shared. It is not assumed to be the basis for further dialogue either by the person who writes the text or the person who receives it. Of course, contributors, when rejected, are expected by those who reject them to possess a certain understanding about the magazine in question, or about the loftier meaning of the whole enterprise of publication. It could be argued that academics can be expected to have such an understanding more than most. So, for example, I can appreciate the generosity of an editor's recent letter that accompanied an extremely full reader's report. The editor mentions that she does not endorse all the report's "sometimes harsh" criticism. She continues: "I hope you understand the spirit in which I send these comments to you."

I do. I think. It's probably best for me not to fret that the spirit may be dead to the letter after all, even for an occasion of such unusual care. I don't feel as excluded being rejected by *Feminist Studies* as I do being rejected far more summarily by the *New Yorker*. Yet in rejection there is always little consolation, and much ignorance. I'll never learn whether my lack of focus was found to be more decisive for the evaluation of my discussion than the absence of gay writers mentioned. And I can't know if my words were felt not to fit with the whole "spirit" of the magazine, even if my footnotes were in order and all the right critics were cited.

At least I didn't get a rejection form only. Many strictly academic periodicals, however, issue only these. Especially because the forms, like memos, or even letters of resignation, comprise one of the ways in which academic life participates in larger conditions of textual production, I want to trace how the whole formal enterprise of rejection eventually brings the following result: a prospective contributor to a magazine, whether an academic or not, is finally a member of no community at all. Instead, he or she has far more in common with the undifferentiated category of a consumer, who knows specifically very little about how any one product comes into being.

The difference is that the contributor, unlike the consumer, is expected to care, whether his or her relation with a specific magazine is civil or not. But how to care? Russell Jacoby suggests that the elaborate acknowledgments to be found today in "serious nonfiction books" have the following rationale: "the author or book passed the test, gaining the approval of a specific network, which filtered out the unkempt and unacceptable."[5] What if you are not in the network? Indeed, what author of an unsolicited manuscript is? No rejection communication of any kind is going to be very forthcoming regarding so much as the existence of such a network. The contributor is going to be left at the end in the same subjugated, voiceless position as the beginning. I want to trace how this position comes about by considering three formal moments in the rejection process: the inscription of something personal on rejection forms, the inclusion of reader reports with rejection letters, and the example of personal communication between editors and contributors.

℞

One never wants to read a rejection form with complete cynicism. Just because each form states the same thing to everybody does not mean it might not be true. Perhaps the editors of the journal who returned my manuscript without postage, above, really did treat my manuscript with great care. Most likely, though, they did not—if only because they could not, with so many other manuscripts pouring in. But then how to comprehend a personal note on the form?

Written at the bottom of the above rejection was the following comment: "interesting piece," signed "all the best" by the editor. Why did he write this comment? In order to take the hard edge off the form? But then if an "informal" comment can so easily be added, what kind of substance does the form have in the first place? It's one thing to extend the import of a rejection form, and another thing, I think, to undermine it.

I'm not sure a personal note ever expects any contributor to tell the difference. Or even to care much about what the note says. Am I entitled to wonder, for example, if "interesting" means "not interesting *enough?*" Or if "interesting" is one of the editor's code words for "good?" Alas, in my own personal coding, something is "interesting" when I really don't know what else to say about it. Should I then read "interesting" to mean "boring?"

But why go on? If the rejection form itself neither asks to be read in this way nor survives such a reading, the editor's note means to be recognized as signifying the same message in a slightly different register: a manuscript has been received and evaluated. If the difference is that I'm being asked to appreciate the *fact* of personal notation itself, I can only reply that rejection forms exist in the first place in order to avoid problems implicit in making some sort of personal contact.

If a magazine chooses to represent itself by a rejection form, the trick may lie in how felicitously the illusion of any personal contact is avoided. Take the following paragraph from the form sent by *Harper's:* "There is no graceful way to return a manuscript with a printed form, but the great

Chapter Three / 58

number of manuscripts we receive makes it impossible for us to thank you personally for your submission." This seems to me a model of its kind. Something that can't be said is nevertheless inscribed. Yet there's one problem: the form is signed, by an editorial assistant.

Does it matter more who signs the rejection form, or if anybody does? It would be worth investigating the historical moment when what are termed in Jack London's *Martin Eden* "rejection slips" began to pass out of standard use in American publishing. Certainly there is no better narrative in American literature about the agony of trying to get published than London's novel (1908). Before Martin begins to make a few sales he has to endure a long period of complete rejection. One day a rejection slip seems to him "so tactfully worded that he felt kindly toward the editor."[6]

It seems clear that this "slip" is not standardized. An editor not only signed the slip but produced it. Martin's distress, however, is not really assuaged when he's finally able to meet an editor. Then he only rages at what he later terms "the inhuman editorial machine." Even if the novel doesn't enable us to recover the moment when slips became forms, it does enable us to see one reason why forms became necessary: to blunt contributorial rage. My sense is that *any* expression of the "human" by anyone connected with the magazine can spark a disappointed contributor into such a response.

Comments ostensibly meant to express kindness or encouragement seldom, if ever, appear to be made with an awareness that they can be received very differently. Recently a friend who writes fiction got a story back with a rejection form on which the editor had written the following: "What a wonderful story! Send more!" "If she liked it so much," lamented my friend, "why didn't she accept it?" Finally, the comment made him mad. He would have preferred to have received no personal communication at all.

At the other extreme are comments—rare, presumably—designed to elicit anger. By far the most interesting rejection I received while circulating an earlier version of this discussion is the following one from a leading literary review, written on the back of a rejection form that regrets "this impersonal reply":

Dear Terry Ceaser [*sic*],

We have a slot open for a piece on origami or interior gardening (focus on use of shiny stones). Your piece would have to be completely rewritten to fill the bill. But don't lose heart. In '78 we received a piece on llama-herding. It just happened to work well with our "Middle Eastern Herding Practices" issue. We printed a vastly edited section of the piece.

From the anonymity of the reader's desk,
[name deleted] (Assistant Editor)

Perhaps these words were designed to amuse rather than provoke. My point, in any case, is that such a silly comment (even if meant to be contemptuous) is all of a piece with a flattering one in the text of rejection. Even granting the existence of elusively different conventions governing rejection by magazines which primarily publish creative writing, the occasion seems to me always compromised, unreadable, and hapless when anything is written on a rejection form. It is ultimately better for a magazine that uses a form to let it speak for itself, even if the lesson, repeated over and over in American practice, is that a rejection form cannot be trusted to do so.

Or even, I would argue, if the rejection form has nothing at all to say about a specific manuscript. My own favorite rejection form is one I've received from time to time over a number of years from the *American Scholar:* "Although we have read your article [title] with interest, we are agreed that we cannot make an offer for publication. Thank you, though, for letting us see your work." I suppose I especially like the use of the word "offer" here. It suggests a no-nonsense realm somehow beyond the mere organization or content of a "work," as well as beyond an editor's reasons or taste. What matters is only whether or not something is going to be accepted. Publication is a business.

Once more, no novel in American literature speaks more directly to the crude commercial fact than *Martin Eden.* During one of his more cynical moments, Martin thinks of the process of submission thus: "He folded the stamps in with his manuscript, dropped it into the letter-box, and from three weeks to a month afterward the postman came up the steps and handed him the manuscript. Surely there were no warm, live editors at the other end. It was all wheels and cogs and oil-cups—a clever mechanism operated by automatons."[7] It may be the case that the editor (whether or not he or she is also a prospective contributor elsewhere) is less free from the system than those prospective authors begging entrance into it.

Why add anything at all to rejection forms? Any inscription can be best understood as the desire of an editor to feel warm or alive. The need may be understandable. The words aren't. Editors seriously err when they scrawl something on the form because these forms express the system—that is, publication *as* system, more or less as Martin is persuaded it is. There are of course other ways to think about publication. But rejection forms have at least one happy consequence: they encourage a contributor to consider the business less in terms of individual vicissitudes or personal networks than as a manifestation of sheer energy with its own logic. The point about the "machine" is to *get caught up in it*.

Many unpublished writers simply refuse to see publication in this way. Instead they take every rejection personally and brood for months before trying again. I have never forgotten a poet I once knew who addressed two envelopes to two separate magazines before he sent out one submission. When he received a rejection form, he simply submitted the unworthy poem to the second magazine, although not before addressing still another envelope first. Not for him cries and whispers, or the rhetoric of regrets and apologies. I did not know the man long enough to observe how often he got published.

He did not care what anybody said. It sufficed for him to be informed that we "can't use" something, that it's "not right for us," or that it "does not fill our current publishing needs." I have always imagined this poet declaring that all reasons for rejection were dull and unsatisfying. Granted, some reasons are more agreeable than others, and it may be that courtesy is never wasted. Yet better the crudest acceptance, I hear the man saying, than the most eloquent rejection. I suppose I could claim that the *cleanest* rejections I've ever received were the two times articles were returned because the respective magazines had ceased publication.

Editors who write on rejection forms just smudge up the works. Apart from rare cases where rejection means informing someone that the mechanism has ceased to function, few editors are going to be able to write anything in a sentence or two either candid or useful. Come to this, how often, in the end, no matter how much or how little energy has been expended on the part of all concerned, is the process of submission even very interesting in some representable way? Another rejection form of which I'm especially fond is a postcard from THE EDITOR that states as follows: "As a matter of policy, *The New York Times Book Review* does not accept unsolicited reviews. Please know, though, that we very much appreciate your interest."

Some time ago I received a rejection letter from the editor of *College English* that gave the following objection: "Our readers found the piece interesting and provocative, but felt that *CE* should not be party to spreading so cynical a perspective on the profession." Fair enough. I refused to swallow the reasoning, but at least I felt I had the indigestible fact served up whole. Rejection letters, unlike forms, give you the impression that you haven't been so much evaluated as recognized, and so judged.

In the above instance I failed to feel outraged. After all, a magazine published by the National Council of Teachers of English has every right to presume its centrality for the profession. Moreover, surely *some* perspectives on it can at least in theory be judged by any organization to be too cynical, or just cynical. Granting all this, however, I couldn't shake off anger. Eventually I figured out why: the presence of those readers.

The editor's judgment is presented as that of the readers. Readers are so common as to be indispensable in academic journals—and some learned journals in all disciplines now impose submission fees (including a mandatory subscription), largely to subsidize the cost for readers to evaluate manuscripts.[8] But the institution of readers presents the contributor with a whole host of problems in understanding a rejection letter. Not the least of them are the ways an editor can represent her own authority in terms of readers.

According to the conventions of any single magazine, how fully must editorial authority defer to that of readers? Are there journals in which the editor can exercise a contrary voice, and prove decisive? Of course such not entirely hypothetical questions can be multiplied. Are there magazine editors, for instance, more akin to the directors of university presses, whose decisions must be confirmed by editorial boards? From the standpoint of a mere contributor, anything collective about a magazine's decision-making is most vexing. Any one reader's report testifies to the presence of collective authority without clarifying it, neither in terms of other readers nor of the editor.

Magazines have different conventions regarding the communication of these reports. Some editors quote from them in their own letters, while others include one whole report or even two in addition to a personal letter. But whatever the convention, there is one especially interesting fact for a contributor, whenever anything at all is communicated (or merely, as above, referred to). No reader can be directly addressed. Readers are, by definition, anonymous. Only the editor has a name.

A friend of mine was furious recently to have had "passed on" by the editor of a journal a reader's report that judged her interpretation of a novel as "just plain wrong." "How can somebody get away with saying this anymore?" she cried. "Hasn't this person learned anything from all sorts of recent theory?" She was angry enough to write a witty rejoinder to the reader through the editor. But of course it was not the same thing. Recalling the rejection of his first manuscript book of poems by a university press (in which his working-class background was utterly dismissed), Paul Mariani concludes: "It's good that such university reviews are anonymous, for I still find myself wanting to smash that blank and stupid face."[9]

If somebody's signature or note troubles a rejection form by casting a beam of something personal on something impersonal, the citation or inclusion of a reader's report in a rejection letter illuminates it in the opposite way: by employing the presence of something expert, objective, and impersonal in a text of something personal. Granted, a reader's report can be (as the one accompanying my letter from the editor of *Feminist Studies*, quoted earlier) "of help." But how, exactly? The most telling example I know may be of a man who was so impressed with the exceptionally lengthy report he received that he imported it whole into his article and rather quickly got it accepted by another magazine.

That is, an anonymous reader's report presumes to be so authoritative as to be definitive. From a contributor's point of view the report begs, often at some variance with the editor's letter, to be accepted entire or not at all. Therefore one's response to an editorial judgment is quite different than to a reader's report. Let me give two examples. The editor of one journal writes that an essay of mine "was too much of a scatter-shot approach," with the "complex positions of other writers too simplified, even misrepresented." No reader's report is mentioned. In contrast, the editor of another journal provides a reader's report in which it is stated as follows: "I cannot shake the conviction that her argument . . . is fundamentally misconceived." And then on for an impressively argued page. The editor seems to concur.

Although I suppose I prefer the second judgment to the first insofar as I can learn from, and even use it in rewriting my essay, the subjective energies still bother me because they're attached to no name. Because of that anonymity, the reader is able to swing free of the very thing the editor, on the other hand, takes for granted, and expects me to as well: his evaluation is impressionistic and personal. If I want to go on and ask whether the editor's letter or the reader's report has more authority in some larger sense of a professional community, I don't know how to adjudicate the matter at all. Had the editor included a weaker reader's report, or had the reader's report been included by a stronger editorial letter, I might have been utterly confounded. Such dissonances happen all the time.

The only consolation the profession gives me is the stability of the reader's report itself. Even if it is almost always offered in conjunction with an editor's letter, the report has the nominal status of a separate document. Reader's reports are necessary because they are objective, and they are objective because they are anonymous. Confronted with a series of rejection letters from various sources, however, any contributor would be forgiven, I think, for being unable to shake the suspicion that reader's reports are necessary because they are anonymous, and they are anonymous because otherwise they would be subjective. To fight through all the wheels and cogs to some contact with this subjectivity is almost impossible. The story of the publication of *Under the Volcano* deserves to be better known in this connection. After the publisher had included a reader's report with his rejection letter, Malcolm Lowry tried to kill himself. Failing, he wrote an enormous rejoinder to the report, and eventually got the novel accepted.

Another story (albeit a theoretical one) about professionally sanctioned anonymity is better known to some academics, as told from the position of the contributor rather than the reader. In his argument against the Modern Language Association's policy of "blind submission," whereby an author's name does not appear on anything submitted to the organization's most prestigious journal, *PMLA*, Stanley Fish concludes that the objectivity is a professional fiction. As for the rationale of "intrinsic merit" constituting the sole criterion of acceptance or rejection, Fish contends that there is no such thing. A great number of professional conventions are always in place, encompassing everything from footnote form to changing fashions. Indeed, there simply *is* no profession apart from these conventions, and intrinsic merit merely abides as one of them, while the very nature of the "intrinsic" keeps changing, as it must, over time.

"The pure case of a reading without bias is never available," concludes Fish, "not because we can never remove all our biases but because without them there would be nothing either to see or to say."[10] I don't cite Fish primarily to agree or disagree with him. My point instead is that his so-phisticated, theoretically nuanced critique takes place at great remove from the ongoing, mundane business of evaluating writing for publication. Even in an academic context, practical urgencies are never dispelled. For journals and magazines that employ readers, individuals must be found for future issues, and trusted to file their reports responsibly and promptly. How many periodicals or readers can afford to proceed with a critique such as Fish's in mind? It suggests no guidelines for the consideration of any one specific manuscript.

On the contrary, readers have been institutionally empowered only to decide if a manuscript is worth publishing. A critique of this power is beside the practical point. Of course, from a less practical vantage, it is easy to see that part of the reason readers have to remain in place to render their decisions is so that contributors stay in place to receive them. The only authority contributors are left with to challenge the inflexibility of each position is that of their own isolated experience—which is precisely the opposite of the sort of authority, at once impersonal and implicitly collective, that readers claim in their reports.

It seems to me important to observe, on the contrary, that reader's reports comprise some of the most biased, self-righteous, and even vicious responses imaginable.[11] Indeed, one function of the accompanying letter from the editor is often—as in my first example given at the outset—to assure a contributor of something more overtly and less harshly personal: no harm was meant, and good will eventually come. But no editors would be likely to open up the magazine's files in this regard to a contributor who requested them.

In his book, *Education without Compromise*, William D. Schaefer appears to draw from some sort of official file in order to give examples of readers' comments during his tenure as editor of *PMLA*. One wishes he had explained his policies. Did he include in his own letter to the would-be contributor the fact that the reader had found the paper "preposterous?" Did he, in another case, provide the report concluding that the submission "cannot help either [the author] or any other scholarly journal that would consider publishing it?"[12] Reports such as these are undoubtedly occasions of some delicacy for editors, who are likely to have seen worse comments from readers than any one contributor ever sees.

Finally, I do not think a stable relationship can be posited between editorial letters and reader's reports. H. L. Mencken somewhere calls criticism "formalized prejudice." My sense is that the institution of the reader's report aims to present the form with the prejudice removed. It is entirely a matter of personal taste whether the editor restores the prejudice once more, by complying with or apologizing for what has not been removed, or else just resorts to some more neutral mediation between reader and contributor. My larger point is a simple one: the exact nature of any one relation between report and letter is less significant than how the respective energies represented by each prove once again impossible to disassociate, and incompatible to co-exist.

Furthermore, the fact that readers never have signatures, whereas editors always do, continues the logic of mechanism. Readers are not, in Martin Eden's word, "automatons." But they are so "cleverly" embedded in the system of scholarly publication that having to remain nameless gives them the character of disembodied beings who cannot be spoken to by any contributor. How much does this matter? It matters as much as the possibility of dialogue does in any human enterprise. To say that an enterprise is mechanistic is in a sense to say that it abides without dialogue.

Finally, in the system of publication, there remains only the editor. The editor represents the human, personal voice who can't or won't be banished. He scribbles a kind word on a rejection form. She writes an encouraging paragraph in a rejection letter after referring to a reader's report. Consequently, it is all the more strange to see what happens when there are no rejection forms or reader's reports, and instead the editor chooses to write directly to a contributor.

What happens is a deeper, if more soft and subtle, fall into what can still be called mechanism. The essence of what the editor will usually write is that there is nothing personal involved: the backlog is too big, the magazine just doesn't consider a particular subject, a new policy is getting established, and so on. In my experience, the more full or even eloquent the personal reply, the more an editor is likely to state that, alas, there are forces beyond anyone's control, even if this comes to mean standards that must be kept up or assignments previously made.

In his new collection of humorous columns from *Grants Magazine, The Grants World Inside Out,* Robert Lucas mentions a Chinese economics journal that handled "wacky ideas" by sending the following form letter:

We have read your manuscript with boundless delight. If we were to publish your paper, it would be impossible to publish any work of lower standard. And as it is unthinkable in the next thousand years we shall see its equal, we are, to our regret, compelled to return your divine composition and to beg you a thousand times to overlook our short sight and timidity.[13]

If one could survey the rejection notices across the country for all magazines of any sort at all, how many would be found regularly to send out "wacky" notices such as this? My guess would be very few. Rejection is serious business. Magazines don't customarily play with authority. Nor are they accustomed to having their authority played with. Consider the poet Robert Wexelblatt mentions in *Professors at Play*, who got so tired of rejection letters that he mimeographed a letter of his own that began as follows: "I am sorry to have to send you this form letter, but I receive so many rejections that I am unable to answer each of them personally."[14]

The idea of replying to a rejection form is of course so funny because it reinstitutes the presence of the personal that the form is designed to ignore. Yet another way to understand the humor is suggested by James Scott, who begins his study of power relations in their textual forms with the following generalization: "the greater the disparity in power between dominant and subordinate and the more arbitrarily it is exercised, the more the public transcript of subordinates will take on a stereotyped, ritualistic cast."[15] In the script of publication, the role of the contributor, upon receiving a rejection notice, is to accept the verdict and not write back.

In Scott's terms, few endeavors—besides the writing of dissertations— demonstrate a disparity of power more than the submission of manuscripts. The contributor is completely subordinated to the authority of the magazine. This is not only why the contributor doesn't write back upon rejection but why he or she has already written such a formal—not to say formulaic—cover letter upon submission. Letters back to contributors from editors, however, would seem to be more relaxed. Personal letters scale down the ceremony to where inequality can be set aside, at least for the occasion of a direct, private communication.

The trouble with such an assumption, though, is that it doesn't work out this way in practice. Above all, contributors are imperiled by mentioning anything mechanical or arbitrary about the business of publication. I was reminded of this a while ago when I received a rejection letter from an editor. Months before, in a fatigued mood, I'd written him a cover letter in which I had referred to "the game of submitting articles." Now, in the course of an unusually generous, careful rejection, he quoted my phrase in order to chastise me for some penciled markings he couldn't ignore in his reading, as well as occasional verbal errors, one garbled sentence, and a stray quotation mark.

I decided to reply to the editor and thank him for what must be, I said, the thankless task of having to write such letters. I didn't refer to the "game" again, nor try to explain any of the literalities he'd mentioned (including those penciled marks, which, truth to tell, had remained from a previous editor's rejection). My place, I think, was to defer to the authority of the editor, who had discreetly put me where I belonged by suggesting that if I was going to see through the game, I had better have mastered all the fundamental rules. For me to point out to the editor that another could easily have ignored the things he mentioned, or even have accepted the article, would have been to try to play a different game.

What are its rules? I'm still not sure. The position of an unsolicited, rejected contributor commands no authority. Nor does it provide any particular vantage point from which to begin some discourse about the follies of acceptance. I've had an essay accepted for publication that was rejected at least ten times, a few of those by magazines less distinguished than the one that eventually accepted it. One of the best journals in the field once accepted another article I had worked myself into enough poise to submit to it, after the thing had been rejected by half a dozen lesser places. All writers have such stories.

But no one editor wants to hear them. What must be rejected above all along with any one manuscript, no matter how reluctantly, is any expression about the ultimate arbitrariness of rejection itself. In my experience, the worse the editor, the more inconceivable the arbitrariness. Twenty years ago I decided to submit a short paper to *Denver Quarterly*. I remember less why I chose this particular journal than why I emboldened myself to submit the piece at all: one of the profession's most eminent professors had nodded approvingly when I presented the discussion to him at the end of a summer postdoctoral seminar. Some people are so afraid of rejection that they never submit anything without someone else's authority.

In any case, I was so unsure of mine, along with being so reluctant to confront the disparity in power mandated by the occasion, that I disdained even typing the cover letter. Instead, I just addressed "Sirs" on a little piece of yellow paper and wrote the following: "I don't know whether you'll consider an article of this sort. Publication, perhaps, is inconceivable. But I do hope you'll consider it." What stance did I think I was taking, what tone did I think I was communicating? I do not remember. If I had not saved the sheet of paper I would not believe now I actually wrote it. The paper was returned to me by the magazine's editor, in an unsealed envelope, along with a rejection form.

On the form the editor typed the following reply: "I find damned little inconceivable. But that a serious magazine should publish what seems to me a graduate school paper—that is, not an essay written out of a fullness of understanding and reflection, but a beginner's probing of new realities— well that is if not inconceivable at least very unlikely." Today the words don't seem so biting. Twenty years ago they were devastating. I still have a copy of a reply, the contemptuous tone of which I tried to fine-tune during more hours than I would care to admit even now. "I see I ought to have adopted a more humble and reverential air," the letter began, "and thanked you for deigning to read my paltry words. It's no worthy explanation, I suppose, to say that out here, beyond the gates, we barbarians do get a little tired of ass-kissing before we're allowed in."

I never sent the letter. I was not afraid. Most likely I just had to face the truth: my most magisterial contempt would merely amount to sour grapes. The editor had all the power. I had none. The state of affairs to which my initial letter was so feebly addressed was given to him to propound, not me. Even if contributor and editor are fellow academics, as we were, they finally share no community at the moment a decision is made to reject a manuscript, because there can be no dialogue between them about it. Further exchanges, as above, are instead merely examples of dominant discourse. A contributor who wants to protest a rejection merely comes out as dominated all over again.

In Scott's terms, the only undominated texts left to the subordinated are what he terms hidden transcripts. A dominant discourse, although not excluded in the same way from having some other outlet, avails itself of hidden transcripts as well—candid, critical writing about the subordinated, circulated intimately in closed circles. Each never reads the hidden transcripts of the other; as Scott states, "the hidden transcripts of dominant and subordinate are, in most circumstances, never in direct contact."[16] What I contemplated doing in my reply to the editor of *Denver Quarterly* was, in effect, making such a direct contact. But it didn't make sense.

What does make sense, I think, at the crucial moment when acceptance or rejection must be decided, is the community of each magazine, defined not so much in terms of how its conventions and values intersect with others but more narrowly in terms of specific networks of affiliation peculiar to itself. It's theoretically possible from the outside to enter one of these communities. All you have to do is submit an article to the magazine, according to the terms of the public transcript. Over acceptance, and then eventually time, you may enter its private conversation, perhaps by being invited to do a book review, or to read some manuscripts, or to meet or talk to the editor on a personal basis. If your manuscript is rejected, on the other hand, you have only the consolations of the hidden transcript, written to your own intimates, and for their eyes only.

What is a magazine's peculiar community? Sometimes it exists on the model of a family. I've known almost half a dozen small magazines where the editor was personal friends with every single contributor. In each case the editor's wife handled more mundane tasks, from proofreading to distribution. Sometimes a community abides on a larger scale, consisting of a number of people held together by common beliefs or convictions. A man who used to write often for a nationally known magazine told me once that regular contributors joked among themselves about representing the last outpost of civilization. But whatever it is, or comes to, a community can't be studied from the outside, in purely textual terms, which is why the *text* of rejection is so elusive, even when an editor writes one personally.

Early in her novel, *Class Porn*, Molly Hite's heroine receives a rejection letter signed by the magazine's managing editor, who adds his initials. "Even the signature has been commercially printed," the heroine thinks. "RP? I think. RP? For some reason it's the initials that outrage me most. It's a little *premature* for initials, I tell myself. They only started publishing last spring. . . . It's a question of status, actually. I was sure they wouldn't reject an article that had both *paradigm* and *topos* in the title."[17] The magazine is already too inward, it appears, presuming a community before establishing a readership. But, once more, how much about a publication's distinctive affiliations can be deduced from a rejection letter?

How many can be expressed? A while ago I knew a couple of women who tried to start a painfully small and obscure literary magazine. They managed to get out two issues in something like a year. One day they received a long piece written in Swahili. It looked like a story. They returned the text, requesting a translation. When it arrived again, the woman were appalled to read what turned out to be the most misogynist drivel. I think they tried to be kind in their rejection letter. But it could not articulate the sort of objection they wanted to make: you either belong to Western civilization or you don't. Just so, people most commonly get rejected, I believe, because finally they either belong or they don't—if not to a group of friends or to an institutional network, then perhaps to a discourse community.

But what is a discourse community? Recently the editor of *College Composition and Communication* called attention in his column to an unsettling new practice: "the small but growing tendency of authors to argue, in later drafts, with comments referees made about earlier drafts of their submissions." Although he professes to not being surprised, given the interest of composition studies in "discourse communities" and "power imbalances of various kinds," the editor worries about the skepticism of those outside the field "about publications that some members of personnel committees may view as defensive or self-congratulatory."[18] In a sense, it turns out that the CCC community has fallen victim to too much discourse, much of it by "unkempt" elements (to recall Russell Jacoby's earlier words) that a stronger network would have kept out.

What sort of a community is a magazine, if one of its own sponsoring subjects (as well as procedures) turns out to be so vulnerable in actual practice? Of course members of such a community can decide that all is "contested" or "problematized" anew, and just continue with the business of publication. What I think the CCC editor's column discloses, however, is that one man's community is another man's publication opportunity. Or, as is usually the case with rejection, one man's publication opportunity turns out to be another magazine's community. From the vantage of the contributor, it is simply not possible to tell beforehand how far down to the communal bedrock even so apparently slight an issue as misspelling will be deemed to go, at least for the immediate purpose of rejection. From the vantage of the editorial board, it may well be the case that rejection provides the best occasion for a magazine not so much to affirm as (re)discover itself.

Of course there are successful magazines that already know who they are, and can afford to flaunt it. Let me conclude with the one time in my life I submitted something to the *New Yorker*. Having returned from a year in Saudi Arabia, still a pretty exotic place in 1982, I thought I had a chance for one of those "Reporter At Large" slots. But I was inexperienced writing journalism. I tried not to make my long account of the kingdom too scholarly. Alas, I was duly rejected. Upon a little slip of paper, an editorial assistant had written: "Unfortunately, your article on Saudi Arabia conflicts with an idea reserved for another writer."

By 1982 I had succeeded in publishing a few things. I felt I could play the game, despite understanding little of the rules. The *New Yorker* rejection showed me how ignorant I really was. My article "conflicts": why yes, I realized. From within the possible publishable discourse about any subject there is bound to be a certain lamentable amount of bumping-into-each-other going on by people who aren't even aware there is anyone else around, until an editor points it out. Who commands a more authoritative view of the comedy than the *New Yorker*? Just as startling was the notion of an idea being "reserved" for another. The rejection didn't forbid me from submitting elsewhere. (I did get the article accepted a year later by the *Yale Review*.) Nonetheless, I should have realized that famous national magazines rarely want unsolicited material. I should have been more mindful that each magazine is its own world, if not community.

I sent the rejection to a friend. He wrote the following series of parodies:

Dear Mr. Caesar:
   Unfortunately, your article on Saudi Arabia does not correspond to the idea assigned to you.

Dear Mr. Caesar:
   We are shocked and alarmed to find that your article on Saudi Arabia expresses an idea reserved for another writer.

Dear Mr. Caesar:
   Your article, which develops Idea ME-SA-R11-433, is not to be written by you, but by another writer. Your correct idea is ME-SA-R11-357, and is not to be published by the *New Yorker* at all, but by *Orbis*.

Dear Mr. Caesar:
   Your article on Saudi Arabia appeared in the Spring, 1926 number of the *Kenyon Review*. I am sorry to remind you that you yourself died in 1946, to the great consternation of your many friends and colleagues.

My first thought on reading these parodies was that I ought to send them to the *New Yorker*. But, once again, they are in fact perfect illustrations of the textual category of Scott's hidden transcripts. The parodies are not meant for the eye of the dominant. Their publication would inevitably change their subordinated character—if only by implicitly suggesting a dialogue on an occasion where there is finally only power, and it is only dominant, at least publicly.

Of course the editorial assistant was kind to write something personal to me. It's at once funnier and grimmer that what she succeeds in evoking is the sort of Orwellian condition my friend parodies. Is it the case, though, that the evaluative system of any one magazine is simply not meant for representation within the larger communal structure of society as a whole? How much difference is *behind* the *New Yorker* rejection, compared to the standard one the editor of a now-defunct little magazine used to mail: "You write like your ass chews gum?" Perhaps it's too facile to speak of mechanism. It is just hard to say.

Of course what appears on a rejection notice matters enormously to each contributor. I treasure the short letter I received a few years ago in which an editor of the *Georgia Review* wrote that my submission was "one of those essays that makes me wish I were an editor of more than one magazine." But I think the essence of any notice is what can't appear, which is the fateful truth that a magazine is, alas, only itself. What precisely does this mean? At least one thing insofar as publication is concerned: the shifting, obscure background of potential contributors (readers of the magazine or not) who have to be rejected are comprehended only with respect to their individual isolation. No less than persons enmeshed in circumstances of sexual harassment or individuals imperiled in the process of dissertation writing, the contributor to a magazine is not a subject of interest in his or her own right, and authorizes no community at all.

Recently *Harper's* published as one of its "Readings" (a feature of the magazine in which hidden transcripts, in Scott's sense, are regularly exposed) a letter from Norman Maclean written in 1981 to an editor at Knopf. After the success of *A River Runs through It and Other Stories*, Knopf wanted to publish Maclean's next book. Apparently it had taken him some time to realize that the editor with whom he had been corresponding worked for the publisher who had fatefully rejected his last book because of the vulgar judgment: it wouldn't sell. Then Maclean was, as he writes, quick to recognize that suddenly he enjoyed "the opportunity of seeing the dream of every rejected author come true." "I am sure," he continues, "that under the influence of those dreams, some of the finest fuck-you prose in the English language has been composed but alas, never published."[19]

How could it be published? If it were published, one could say, it wouldn't be subordinated. Moreover, it couldn't be published because the whole logic of "fuck-you prose" is that it is only written as a condition of being unpublishable. Finally, because the occasion is rejection, publication is of course logically impossible anyway. And yet *Harper's* makes the impossible dream come true, truer than Maclean could have dreamed when he wrote a private letter. The "Readings" note explaining the circumstances of the letter neither explains how the magazine came into possession of it, nor pauses to reflect on how the very fact of publication so curiously belies the exquisitely personal conditions of its very writing.

After ruminating over his embarrassment at not having noticed his man's stationery sooner, Maclean concludes as follows: "However, having let the great moment slip by unrecognized and unadorned, I can now only weakly say this: if the situation ever arose when Alfred A. Knopf was the only publishing house remaining in the world and I was the sole surviving author, that would mark the end of the world of books." Of course no one can judge that what Maclean concludes to the Knopf editor represents the dream of anyone who has ever been rejected by a magazine or a publishing house. All one can say is that for one textual moment a hidden transcript participates in dominant discourse. Boundaries have shrunk to a community of two. Upon someone who has been rejected has been bestowed the power to reject in turn, and an author who has been pronounced stillborn into the world of books gets to enact a fantasy of having the power to pronounce this same world at an end because he will publish no more.

Chapter Four

The Green Bean Campaign

in the Memo

Nancy Miller has an essay on her career, which had the following development when she became the director of the Women's Studies Program at Barnard: "I wrote a book-length collection of memos, characterized by the rhetorical turns of feminist righteousness, in a mode a colleague from Political Science taught me called 'bullets'; my memo style, she explained, was too narrative."[1] From this comment we can learn at least three things about memos:

1. Memos are ephemeral. Miller will never publish them in a book. Nobody would want to read them.
2. Memos are the product of various discourses. Like any writing, a memo has a particular rhetoric, which can be distinguished from other rhetorics.
3. Memos have generic forms. Depending on the occasion, some forms are better than others.

There is probably also a fourth thing: your academic career is going to be representable in terms of memos, whether or not it proves to be better (Miller doesn't say for her part) to give than to receive.

What is a memo? I have at hand one from the vice president for student affairs at my university to the "University Community" in which he states that, before anyone could "utilize" the food service, a Catering Service Form must first be completed at his office. If all memos merely presented information in this way, there would appear to be no need to pose questions about them. "Every established order tends to produce (to very different degrees and with very different means) *the naturalization of its own arbitrariness*," writes Pierre Bourdieu.[2] Memos feel so natural to receive in any university that few people who do not even know about the housing service, and do not care about the Student Affairs Office, wonder nonetheless why they should be bothered to read such a memo in the first place.

Every institutional structure may be more than the sum of its memos. And yet there is a very real sense in which the structure is cemented, day by day, department by department, out of hundreds and thousands of sheets of paper circulated as agreeably as air-conditioned air in summer or heat in winter. Memos comprise the preeminent example of an unexamined textual practice in the academy today. They are unexamined because they are practical. Yet the converse is more provocatively true: memos are practical because they are unexamined.

In one of the few considerations of memos that I know of—in a section entitled "The Memorandum as Act," on *The Pentagon Papers*—Richard Ohmann states the following: "The writers of memoranda sit on the stream of events and try to direct it. They employ power directly."[3] The most intriguing thing about memos as a textual practice is that they express power so immediately, ceaselessly, and bluntly they hardly seem like "texts" at all. The vice president of student affairs is in charge of the food service. Who can dispute it? Therefore the vice president is authorized to disseminate rules concerning the food service. Who would want to challenge his authority to do so? The claim of memos to be purely factual follows directly from the unquestioned status of the power they exercise.

Consequently, the first thing one notices in considering memos as texts is the more curious: few are content to be "purely" factual. Ones that are have to do with time: Friday is "Black Friday" of National Collegiate Alcohol Awareness Week, the Sabbatical Leave Committee will hold a Question-and-Answer session on a certain date, the Writing Across the Curriculum committee presents a lecturer, and so on—just to take some examples from my own university during a typical year. If the most basic function of a memo is to *announce* something, the announcement is most factual when the appointment of an executive assistant to the dean or the Valentine's Day carnation sale can be presented as a strictly temporal thing.

However, most memos cannot limit themselves in this way. Even the one cited above on the food service has another paragraph in which it is explained that the university food service contractor cannot be contacted directly for use of its facilities; instead, all such business must proceed through Student Affairs. So it goes with most memos. The most apparently factual information turns out to require some form of explanation or justification. Indeed, such justification, most commonly, is the actual rationale for the memo, and not merely the specific announcement.

From the perspective of its memos, any institution's power is not self-evident. It has to be made good—less arbitrary—in hundreds of trivial ways. Even the simplest temporal facts need reiteration ("just a reminder") and hardly any information can be disseminated without consolidating why it is important in the first place or how it fits into some larger network of regulation, law, and policy. It does not suffice for Printing and Duplicating to state that direct single copies from bound books will no longer be made. The memo must speak of budget constraints and copyright laws. We need to inquire whether this interest of memos in their own legitimation reveals a politics of memo writing.

Memos are nothing if not, in James Scott's sense, *public* transcripts, and therefore are written by the members of what he would term dominant groups. Subordinate groups *are* subordinate because they do not write counter-memos objecting to the food service policy of Students Affairs or the copy procedures of Printing and Duplicating. Moreover, what could be written by anyone in response must conform to the character of the public transcript. Later, I will try to show how parodies of memos are especially clarified by Scott's study of textual hegemony.[4]

However, their repeated writing-out of the grounds for their own authority discloses that the kind of social and political control memos aim to accomplish is not ultimately the result of disparity in institutional power. Some of the peculiar logic of memos has to do with sheer organizational size, confusion, or overlap. The relation between Student Affairs and Printing and Duplicating is not one of hierarchy. It is hard to say what the relation is (if any), and much easier for each department just to write a memo to the other, as well as everybody else. Nonetheless, I will be more interested during the following discussion in texts where an organizational hierarchy is presumed to be in place and where some decisive boundary between dominant and subordinate groups is marked.

Finally, what I hope to demonstrate is that even in such cases each category can be studied as being in more direct contact with the other than the boundary between them would seem to allow. Memos comprise a remarkably varied, heterogeneous textual practice because the institutional politics, or micro-politics, they reflect are not stable. Whether it has to do with investigating charges of sexual harassment or instituting procedures for completing a dissertation, power in a university structure most especially remains to be implemented and performed as a condition of its being rationalized.[5] The rationalization opens up the memo to the very energies that Scott studies as hidden.

Of course any single memo continues to abide as the premier text of bureaucratized, technocratic control. Modern work has long been work that has to include the expectation of memos. And yet I will maintain that even in the rhetoric there is more "heteroglossia" that has to be accommodated than technical or officialized rules would seem to stipulate.[6] Memos are obsessed with language. They often originate because a word or a phrase has been misunderstood, or because a new policy objective or procedural matter has to be clarified on an ostensibly semantic level. Words such as "disabled" or "interdisciplinary" gain a place in a professional lexicon only with struggle. Arguably, memos spend just as much time admitting words into a particular professional discourse as they do excluding them.

Furthermore, considered strictly as texts (and in great contrast to rejection letters), memos have to be unusually intimate with the sources of their own critique. Some of these are outward. Everyone knows of cases when the broad public terms of a memo conceal a personal grievance on the part of the person who wrote it against someone else. (I know a woman who swears her supervisor once observed her laughing and proceeded to write a memo to the staff about professional behavior.) Some of the sources are inward. How personal should the writer anticipate objections about a memo will be, and how unselfconscious about this is it best to appear? A few years ago I heard of a dean who used to write regular memos defending himself against the critical reception of the last memo.

But whether a memo originates as a critique or becomes an object of critique, it is easy to see how its own authority as a public transcript is open to hidden ridicule. I believe the nature of this ridicule is a cardinal fact about the politics of memos, and in the final section of my discussion I want to consider the moment of parody in the memo. Memos are parodied for a number of reasons—some having to do with their own dynamics as texts, and some with their peculiar function as political acts within organizations. In any case, it may be ultimately in their parodies that memos are saved, perhaps even more than they are damned, by people who want to save themselves from memos, once they understand that control of even the most minimal means of representation shapes the nature of experience itself.

೪

During one recent year at my university a document appeared entitled, "Summary of Open CCPS [Committee on Courses and Programs of Study] Hearings on the Recommended General Education Program." Such documents—not to say such hearings—are of course the staple of academic business-as-usual: programs need continually to be readjusted, made subject to recommendations, and launched into the next decade, if not the next century. This particular document is what could be classified as a report or position statement rather than a memorandum or a memo.

The differences are instructive. I don't think that finally there are any worth insisting upon between a memorandum and a memo. A memo aspires to the condition of a memorandum, which is a more comprehensive and self-sufficient account of its own conditions, including the need for its very production. Some difference between a report or position statement and a memorandum, on the other hand, is worth at least supposing, because the former has a more decisive relation to the conditions that summon it into existence. Ohmann gives a common, general rationale: "By meetings, memoranda, and allied forms, the members of an organization try to grasp the import of past events and to exercise a measure of control over future events."[7] The grasp of the position statement, however, so takes possession of a particular occasion that its publication becomes an "event" in its own right.[8]

The one cited above authorizes itself to respond to objections to its recommended program—and these responses, in turn, become part of the program. Doubts had been expressed about certain "gaps" in the earlier recommendations. The Summary is not happy with these "gaps," continually referring to them in quotation marks in the process of explaining that in fact "these definitional 'gaps' were explicitly acknowledged in the document." The very word "gap" has apparently caused some offense.

This rhetorical situation is very typical of public transcripts. Some problem of a more obscure or private nature has arisen that must be taken into account, and the available vocabulary has no convenient name for it. What to do? The most common solution is to adopt an alien word usage, thus reinstituting part of the very problem. But the offending word is framed by quotation marks. As much as any other discursive strategy, the use of quotation marks casts a rhetorical pall on the objection, which can then be rewritten in more acceptable language, or else transformed in more comprehensive ways. Hence, the Summary concludes its consideration of "gaps" thus: "The definitional 'gaps' for the writing intensive 'WI' flagged courses have been formulated by the University Writing Across the Curriculum Committee, and are attached at Appendix B."

Yet slang, idiom, and all manner of everyday, conversational usage are read out of the public transcript neither so easily nor so uniformly. Another institution's Summary might have used the word "gaps" without quotation marks. Still another might have taken to the word as if it were its own very music, as the word "flagged" evidently is heard here. Or consider the Summary's use of the word "grandfathered," as in the following statement: "these courses would be 'grandfathered' in without formal review." The first use of the word is in quotation marks. The second use refers, without quotation marks, to "this grandfathering process," but a third instance of the word, in the very next sentence, features quotation marks once more.

Reports or position statements draw from a fund of rhetorical and formal operations they have in common with memoranda and memos. A more extensive, encompassing practice (the document from which I am quoting consists of twelve pages) shows, I hope, more vividly how insecure all public transcripts are with choices of diction, not to mention other stylistic options. Thus, a memo from the coordinator of student activities puts "and," "hold," and "official" each in quotation marks. Why? It might not be so easy to see apart from context, but the reason is the same as why the CCPS position statement stumbles over "gaps" and wavers before a "grandfathered" procedure: neither text, no matter how different with respect to institutional function, is self-sufficient. Therefore each occupies a position of perpetual instability about how seriously its lack of self-sufficiency should be understood.

The best solution is to leave the decision to somebody else. I think the following statement can be proposed as a general rule: the shorter the public transcript, the more like a dialogue. The longer, the more autonomous, and therefore like a text. Memos comprise a heterogeneous formal practice because any one example can devolve back into the institutional forest from which it emerged or evolve into the more specialized hothouse growth proper to a memorandum. Both directions can take place in the same document. We have all read memos which conclude thus: "In addition, we are always looking for new ways to publicize activities and/or to elaborate on the content of the programs being scheduled so please call our office if you have suggestions that we might use or pass on to sponsoring organizations." Nothing guarantees, though, that there have not been preceding paragraphs whose vocabulary is safely distant from anything oral: "The University Special Projects program is designed to encourage and support special projects at State System of Higher Education universities intended to enhance the quality of teaching and learning at the university and to contribute to the professional development of faculty members involved and/or affected by the project."

Another way to characterize the formal variety of memos would be to claim that nothing prevents a memo from developing into a memorandum. Even a memo whose message is, *please disregard the previous memo*, will not necessarily forgo arguing the case rather than merely declaring it. Consider a mistake on an examination schedule or an incorrect procedure to record final grades. Neither has to be necessarily explained by the registrar as having had to do with computer error, recent changes in staff, or anything else. Why make some explanation anyway—promising, in conclusion, to rectify the problem or to update the files while appreciating the patience of all faculty in the meantime? I believe the answer depends upon how much reciprocal action is expected by those who send a memo from those who receive it.

Some texts beg only to be read. (Or remembered, to recall the derivation of the word "memo" from the Latin *memorare*, "let it be remembered.") Others imagine a more active response—most conventionally, further questions that require actual contact with whoever sent the memo. Hence, memos usually conclude with a phone number, thereby reengaging the ground of dialogue in which they were conceived. Memoranda, on the other hand, tend to discourage some further response, even if a phone number (or a deadline of some sort) is attached at the end. Often, the difference is not so much one of form or length as of tone. A recent article on the great Indian scientist and administrator, Homi Bhabha, quotes a memo of his dealing with the attitude staff is expected to have toward the buildings and grounds of the institute Bhabha founded, after which the author comments: "This is not a memo to grown men and women: it is a memo from a father to his children."[9]

In Bhabha's case, the dialogue never got started. Much of the formal variety of memos has to do with the degree of dialogue—to write "dialogic possibility" might be to sound too much like a memorandum—represented in any one. The more dialogue, the more diversity, or at least openness to qualifications, counter views, differences of opinion, and even humor. I've never been in a position to write very many memos myself, and when I was, during a tenure as director of my department's graduate program, the first memo I wrote began with a favorite quotation from Kafka: "The verdict doesn't come all at once, the proceedings gradually merge into the verdict." It didn't take me long to discover that, like Miller's, my "memo style" was too narrative—and too literary. It is necessary to return to the matter of why the literary dimension poses such a scandal in the text of the memo.

Memos proceed by appropriating various levels of language use. Some prove more suitable, or practical, than others. The most powerful influence on memo-writing is exercised by one area: the conversational. Let me illustrate by citing a two-page document my dean sent to the Arts and Sciences faculty, which began by recalling the "dialogue" he had begun with a previous "letter" on the subject of the budget. "We must continue our dialogue" in this period of "diminishing resources," he concludes in the second paragraph. After several more have accumulated (in which we are asked to do such things as rededicate ourselves to our "mission" and reexamine our "priorities") a last flurry of questions suddenly becomes a storm, and the penultimate paragraph reads: "Is the College or the University more than the sum of its departments? Can there be biology without chemistry? Can the arts flourish if the humanities languish?"

These are indeed hard questions. But I don't think the dean expects anybody to answer them. Worse, he appears to be listening only to himself asking them. Notwithstanding the fact that the document calls itself a letter, and speaks through to the upbeat end about dialogue, no space for a reply on the part of some other has been imagined, nor has a need for it been dramatized. The striking thing about the document is its *written* character, which has been purchased by assimilating the form of oral communication wholesale. On the basis of such an example, it would be tempting to say that a memorandum, as distinct from a memo, either represents a failed dialogue, or refers to a dialogue that already took place, but not according to the correct terms, which are stipulated in the memorandum. What the dean means, after all, is that we should be talking about our mission rather than our money.

Certainly memos err, when they do, by ignoring the resistances that may have provoked them, or that may be implicit in them, no matter what they try to communicate. Another example. I have a three-paragraph memo from the State Department, written a decade or so ago. The first two paragraphs explain how the Federal Employee Literacy Training (FELT) program developed from a Reagan policy initiative. The final paragraph begins thus: "If you are interested in volunteering for FELT . . . ." The supposition carries the (FELT) force of an injunction once a reader suspects that the memo is actually about organizational politics and not adult literacy. At this point, the only available position is one of subordination, over against the dominance of the memo itself, whose coercive nature is so complete it doesn't have to be rhetorically acknowledged.

Let me contrast another State Department memo, to Public Affairs officers in diplomatic missions throughout the world, which stages its own rhetorical occasion far more effectively. The subject is a new records system (DRS). "Questions are still coming in from the field," the memo begins, "regarding the treatment of the elite (DRS) as against the mass audience in ICA programs." Of course questions may not be coming in. Indeed, PAOs throughout the world may have already learned to ignore the new DRS, or else to file it away as yet another "program objective" mistakenly mandated from afar. Nevertheless, for the purposes of the memo, it helps to represent PAOs as engaged in active dialogue with Washington, so that a position of dominance doesn't have to be considered, or one of subordination felt.

Does DRS have the status of a favored acronym in the United States Information Service at present? Is it a cliché? Perhaps a metaphor—the name of a brilliant idea or an infamous folly? One studies at some peril the memos of organizations of which one is not a part, realizing that much of the rationale for their texts is to reinstate the very identity of the organization in terms of itself by means of a special vocabulary. One reason for the memo was to define the word, and not merely defend a program. Just so, the reason for the dean's "letter" above was to renew a venerable discourse on higher education, presently endangered by the vulgar matter of the college being underfunded. Memos do not simply enact a contest over who gets to control language. They provide the central textual site within any organization for how power is made manifest.

It must be done with some care. Ineffective memos fall victim to a whole dynamic of dominance, whereby a rhetorical stance has lost touch with the sources of resistance to a word, a subject, or a whole way of thinking. Scott has studied the responses of subordinated groups to the fact that the public transcript has not taken them into account and instead only demonstrated all over again the great disparity of unequal power. Subordinated groups respond with what he terms the hidden transcript—a whole critique of power encompassing rumors, jokes, strategic acts of protest, and so on. The public transcript, in turn, is shaped by the hidden one in constant but elusive ways. Scott claims of the hidden transcript that "the mere fact that it is in constant dialogue—more accurately, in argument—with dominant values insures that hidden and public transcripts remain mutually intelligible."[10]

The reason memos speak so much about "dialogue" is not only because modern forms of social control prevent it. Dialogue keeps the argument open, or, in memo-ese, "ongoing." Dialogue makes it possible for a public transcript to be, exactly, intelligible to those over whom it has authority. Not all of these people are subordinates, or even if, on occasion, they are, not all of the time. Nonetheless, no public transcript is going to be able to recreate all the energies of those whose business it is to read the document. Some energies are always going to remain hidden, and, in Scott's terms, these are the ones—having to do with ignorance, rumor, misunderstanding, and so on—that already exercise a shaping force on the memo. In effect, some of the substance of the hidden transcript is already part of the public one.

Scott puts the matter thus: "The hidden transcript is continually pressing against the limit of what is permitted on stage, much as a body of water might press against a dam."[11] What happens in ineffective memos is that the dam breaks, and all that a reader sees is so much hopeless effort to stop the flow. I have a memo from the personnel director of Voice of America to all Washington employees on the subject of the agency's hazardous weather policy. The text begins by reminding employees that most of them are considered essential, and therefore are required to be at work during emergency situations. Immediately there are at least two problems: how to define "essential" and how to define "emergency." The memo can't do either, and yet proceeds for a page and a half as if it has done both. Essential employees are those who are notified (annually, in writing) that they are. Those who have not been so notified will be "charged" for the leave they will be allowed to take, unless yet another category obtains: "extreme emergency situations." Examples are not given of this last category.

Nuclear war? Armageddon? the friend who sent me the memo wondered in the margin. In his accompanying letter, he wrote a number of other queries about his own "essential" status. His letter to me functioned as the rebuke of a hidden transcript to the memo's public one. The personnel director had the thankless task of having to ignore how some words in some contexts are either haplessly dictatorial, like "essential," or hopelessly superfluous, like "extreme" added to "emergency." In addition, the agency imperative to mandate a "weather policy" had to set aside such unregenerate facts about power relations as that everybody likes to consider his or her job as in some way essential. Furthermore, nobody likes to come to work when the city is covered with snow.

The importance to memos of the whole notion of a dialogue between dominant and subordinate, or public and hidden, can be framed in another way: ineffective memos fail to contain their own implicit parody. Instead, ridicule suddenly appears as if in the form of additional words—the very words, it may be, that the memo was written to counter in the first place. The moment of parody is to the memo as the hidden transcript is to the public one: the subordinated voice of the whole dialogue, whose pressure can be felt but whose words cannot be uttered openly because the representation of the dominant depends upon their not being uttered. In a final section, I want to consider the significance of the subordinated voice when it speaks, in disguise.

❧

One year the Clarion University faculty received the following memo, which I give in full:

> Between April 19th and 23rd, the Office of Alcohol and Drug Awareness Education and BACCHUS will be conducting a green bean campaign. This program includes a series of five posters that will be appearing around campus.
>
> We are asking you to participate by bringing a can of green beans to your class sometime between April 19th and 23rd (just carry it within you if you like green beans). If the students ask you about them just say you like green beans. Only do it if you like green beans. Riverside [market] has donated several cases of beans to us if you need a can.
>
> We want to surprise you with the posters, it is a fun and educational campaign. It has to do with alcohol abuse intervention. We want to keep it a secret for the students. If you would like more information about it to participate, you can call the Alcohol and Drug Awareness Education Office at 2418.

How can we explain such a silly document?

I don't think it suffices to remark on how, once more, the language of dialogue is used to make an empty contact with an audience. What is the memo to say to someone who doesn't like green beans, but still wants to "participate"? Or perhaps somebody who likes only yellow beans? Or just somebody who doesn't see the connection between alcohol and beans? The connection seems so intrinsically frivolous—at least as given here—that a counter voice of some sort seems essential if the memo is to preserve its serious intent.

As it is, the memo is so happily unaware of how it contains within itself the logic for its own subversion—if not mockery—that one could well read it and suspect a parody of a certain sort of excited, pious idealism. The sheer inarguable rectitude of drug awareness does so much rhetorical work that the whole proposal seems deliberately naive. Yet, short of picking up the phone, how to be sure that the memo isn't in fact a parody? I think the only way is to emphasize the importance of another source of authority in the memo: the official office, named both at the beginning and end. In any memo, *origin* is the ultimate guarantor of legitimacy, if not meaning. Considered as a political act, the dissemination of the memo itself is more decisive than its textual form.

Another example. In her presidential address to the American Studies Association a couple of years ago, Martha Banta mentions part of the description of a graduate seminar, "New Historicism for White Boys," that appeared in the faculty mailboxes of the UCLA history department: "This is a course for nice liberal white males who feel politically inconsequential and seek safe ways to alleviate their helplessness and guilt, but all 'others' are welcome to watch them writhe." Banta confidently calls the memo a parody. But since we do not have the full text, I am not absolutely convinced.[12]

However, Banta gives one more piece of information: the course was to be taught by a Professor Blancmange. The most certain way to code a text as a parody is either to spoof its origin or just withhold it. If the document is a memo, the mockery of origin accomplishes an additional thing: to the degree that memos reproduce the organizational structure, that order itself falls under critique. This, in turn, is another reason why little is gained by reading the green bean memo above as a parody. The Alcohol and Drug Awareness Education Office is too inconsequential to be worthy of criticism, much less the peculiar homage that parody pays to authority by imitating it. The UCLA history department, on the other hand, is a more interesting, illuminating upholder of institutional politics, or rather politics as course structure.

It is worth distinguishing between the fact of the memo itself and its particular textual form because many parodies of memos fix only on their origin, as a way of ridiculing the organizational fiat implicitly expressed in any memo, no matter how genuinely issued as a dialogue. Early in Don DeLillo's first novel, *Americana*, the narrator picks up the following memo and reads it:

> To: Tech Unit B
> From: St. Augustine
>   And never can a man be more disastrously in death than when
>   death itself shall be deathless.

It turns out that these memos have been appearing in this particular sub-section of the narrator's business for over a year. "Previous memos had borne messages from Zwingli, Levi-Strauss, Rilke, Chekhov, Tillich, William Blake, Charles Olson, and a Kiowa chief named Satanta." The author of these memos has become known as "the Mad Memo-Writer," but the narrator finds this name too "obvious," and calls him Trotsky instead.[13]

Of course DeLillo's narrator is a shrewder judge than his fellows of the politics of memos. What "Trotsky" is doing is subverting the organizational location of memos by mocking two things in particular about their authority. First, the authority is, in Bourdieu's phrase cited earlier, "unnatural." To be subordinated is to be subordinated to a *site*. To begin to question why a department head is a department head can inexorably lead to more "revolutionary" questions, such as why there is a need for either departments or heads, much less how the issuing of memos reinforces the power of both, ultimately by situating each at the same immemorial location, over and over again.

A second thing Trotsky mocks is harder to stipulate, and has more to do with the fall into textuality that any memo, even the most brief, must endure, if only as a condition of being a written document that has an author. The very idea of St. Augustine or William Blake writing memos is absurd because the only virtues of memo language are local and practical: immediacy, utility, intelligibility, and so on. "Heteroglossia" to the contrary, the openness of a memo at the vernacular end becomes closure at the philosophical end. Memos are about procedures, not ideas. At most, the authors of memos are concerned with implementing things and not philosophizing on them. To put the point too bluntly: the memo is a *stupid* form of textuality, and only its effectiveness as communication within the highly temporal realm of institutional politics ultimately redeems it.[14]

Unless parody does. I have tried to explain parody as a component feature of memos in their character as public transcripts. Scott, however, scarcely mentions parody. His emphasis on the social experience of subordination—defined in terms of submission and indignity—precludes it. Parody suggests not so much more respect for power than the serfs and slaves of Scott's account possess as more detachment from it. Parody registers how the experience of modern forms of bureaucratized control in institutional bodies is finally profoundly different from, say, the social situation of the proletariat in Czarist Russia: the stuff of power is more equitably distributed and better managed ritualistically, even for someone engaged in the production of a dissertation. Indeed, the ease is managed in part through memos, which negotiate the large question of how much power to distribute to subordinates in terms of the small operation of how much power to represent. How much? Just enough, it turns out, at once to engage and contain the argument of the hidden transcript.

Of course much depends upon the exact circumstances of any institution at one point in time. To gloss the whole of an immense textual field encompassing hundreds and thousands of modern organizations and institutions each day is impossible.[15] The very emergence of a memo is a symptom of some dissonance or problem that is often simultaneously created and solved by the memo alone—ideally in a simple and time-bound manner. But gaps among levels of an organization are continually opening up. Neither the most exacting of memos nor the most eloquent of position papers will solve all the dissonances. Moreover, no matter the specific structure of an institutional hierarchy, many groups are always being repositioned in terms of dominant and subordinate positions, sometimes by the very memoranda that attempt to arbitrate among them or declare a dialogue between them.

How regularly in all these myriad work sites do parodies appear? I do not mean parodies that are (or are perceived to be) the product of one individual, but instead parodies that seem to be the product of a species of folk discourse. We have all seen them. They are suddenly sent to us or thrust into our hands, by smiling colleagues who tell us that they got them from someone else, who didn't know or remember how someone else got hold of them. When we read one of these parodies, it ceases to matter who wrote it, because it speaks for us, in our secret heart of hearts—or rather in our collective, subordinated capacity.

Let me cite one that I first read typed on the letterhead stationery of a Pennsylvania university. But the friend who sent it to me received a copy distributed from within her own Pennsylvania community college. To one side of the letterhead, the author of the memo has an individual (fictitious?) name, while on the other side something called the "Faculty Development Committee" has been typed in as the source. The subject of the memo is: Control of Travel Costs. The opening paragraph reads as follows:

> As you are all aware, we are doing our best at this time to control the expenditures of the University so that we can allocate our resources to the most essential things rather than to "extras." I have been long convinced that travel expenses are one area where real savings could be achieved if we put our minds to it. As a result of a lot of creative thinking by the Provost's Council and others, starting immediately, we are instituting the following policies relating to travel on University business.

The first policy considered is transportation. Hitchhiking is the only option for assistant professors. Associates, "under some circumstances," can use buses. Full professors, "with the permission of the President," can use airlines, but only on a discount basis. "If, for example, a meeting is scheduled in Seattle but a discount fare can only be obtained to Detroit, then travel will be sanctioned only to Detroit."

So the document continues. About lodging: "Faculty are encouraged to stay with relatives and friends." Concerning meals: bringing your own food is especially "cost effective," and cans of tuna or pork 'n' beans "can be conveniently consumed at leisure without the unnecessary bother of heating or other costly preparation." There is a concluding "Final Thought": "Let me suggest that departments and centers plan ahead for meetings and conferences and send faculty and students together in small groups. The experience could then become not a mere conference trip but an adventure not unlike the 'wilderness bonding retreats' we read so much about these days. The beauty of this proposal is that people pay good money for these retreat experiences, whereas ours can be had absolutely free."

This parody seems to me an excellent example of how parodies *speak* to power. Legion are the number of memos at all universities each year necessary to set out annual travel policies. And yet how few, if any, succeed in coming to terms with the unwieldy expenses of any individual who sets out conference-ward? What memo on professional travel can gracefully avoid casting all these individuals into a class, all subordinated to an arbitrary, dominant rule that forces one to choose between steak and Spam? The topic of travel costs is one of those subjects that doom an administration to have to legislate quite specifically and to have to endure being resented for it quite generally. To academics at least, the very subject is a ritual one. And so, for this reason, is the mockery.

The above parody is misunderstood if read only as protest. It is just as much play—the explicit portion of a dialogue heretofore conducted only in official transcripts with an anonymous, irreverent, hidden presence which speaks at last in the parody. This presence should be conceived of as always already arguing with official cant of all sorts, and yet so much imbued, if not in love, with cant, that the final suggestion expressed here, converting one form of academic nonsense into another sort, proves irresistible. The parody represents a joyously liberated discourse. But if it were completely uninhibited it wouldn't be a parody because there would be nothing for the discourse to adhere to, or to imitate.[16] Ultimately, I think, the parody is happy to be a memo, and probably more pleased to consider travel costs—or for that matter academic politics—than it can actually represent.

In this, the parody is symmetrical with almost any official memo on travel costs, which is most likely far more unhappy to say anything than it could possibly represent. Indeed, one surmises that a college provost is just about as sadly resigned to writing a memo about travel costs as a personnel director in the federal government is to writing about the weather. Either one would surely rather take up rhetorical arms against the languishing state of the humanities. (A venerable theme unavailable to the editor of a magazine who has to write a rejection letter.) As it is, memos and their parodies provide unusually good examples of how the public transcript and the hidden transcript are each unintelligible without the other.

"The political struggle to impose a definition on an action and to make it stick," writes Scott, "is frequently at least as important as the action per se."[17] I think we can conclude at least two things about memos on the basis of their parodies: first, memos are not disseminated without struggle, and second, parodies of them reveal how the basic political character of memos is the form of an imposition. Once more, I do not mean to imply by this last point that the imposition, any more than the politics, is a uniform thing. Memos may well be more heterogeneous as texts than the organizations within which they operate. Moreover, in their status as documents necessary to maintain day-to-day business-as-usual, most memos already "stick," merely by virtue of their very dissemination.

And yet, do they? The "dialogue" of the memo comes, by definition, preabsorbed, and its re-presentation is the sole province of the dominant class that authorizes the public transcript. This does not mean that in fact dialogue will be impossible; on the contrary, I have tried to show that to a degree the hidden transcript is already present. What I do believe we can conclude is a third thing about memos: parodies of them reveal that we can never know enough about how memos are actually received. This is to say, we do not know enough about institutional politics. In this sense, I endorse a recent proposal by Susan Horton—attempting to discuss the politics of her department's Ph.D. program—that runs as follows: "A Ph.D. in literacy could open up a space in which we could invite literature students who are well-trained in close reading to use their skills on, say, institutional discourse, in a practical course that could combine readings of Foucault, Benjamin, Nietzsche, and Vico . . . with a reading of, say, the language of university memoranda and college course syllabi."[18]

In another sense, however, such a proposal sounds like DeLillo's "Mad Memo-Writer" gone madder—or rather, more academic. She has a Ph.D. now, and her "Trotskyite" energies are displaced beyond recognition. Or anyway safely within politics of a familiar liberal pluralist sort. To dream of St. Augustine and memos on the same agenda is to recreate a model of the school as an institution where even its own ridicule, already ritualistically venerated, becomes a further, deeper basis for subordination to an academic program. Horton's proposal is the sort of thing a would-be parodist would be delighted to try to write up, even knowing full well that Horton, when she reads it, would most likely be pleased to add the parody to her own course syllabus.

Throughout this book I have been suggesting that the dominance of some institutional discourses, such as those about sexual harassment, dissertation advisement, and publication protocols, is so powerful that they cannot finally be publicly written about at all. Or else, if the discourse is a wider one, as with feminism, it may become almost exclusively institutionalized anyway in the process of being formally subjected to critique. In a chapter on gender- and racially-based language reform in his latest book, Russell Jacoby concludes thus: "Without a sure sense of linguistic limits, we are tempted to heal social ills by correcting, revising, and prohibiting language. . . . In easing the pain, decorous talk may forget the disease."[19] But what precisely *is* the disease of the memo? Its burden to represent the very idea of decorous talk?

Perhaps the best one can hope for the politics of memos is to understand their power as the ceaseless, arbitrary imposition of dominant discourse upon recalcitrant, hidden experience. Institutional life is conducted on the basis of memos. And yet this basis is not wholly life, not even in institutions. We might consider the strategy Paul Theroux adopts in having the last two pages of his novel about institutional life at the American Embassy in London, *The Consul's File*, consist of a memo from the narrator to his superiors. The chapter, entitled "Memo," is about the impossible disposition of private sources of emotion within public frameworks of meaning.

The narrator (unnamed throughout until the final page of the novel) does not resign. He has learned too much during the course of the linked stories that comprise the book, and much of his experience is bitter. The narrator could have resigned, of course. Instead, in the memo, he confesses his love for "Subject" (a radical American academic whom he has met at a diplomatic party a couple of chapters before) and reports on the fact of his marriage in the last few lines. As he begins his memo: "When I took up my post at the London embassy I entered into a tacit agreement to share all the information to which I became privy that directly or indirectly had a bearing on the security of the United States of America or on my own status, regardless of my personal feelings."[20]

By the conclusion, though, so much fugitive personal feeling has found its way into the transcript that the form has come to seem empty and artificial. The diplomat's words are by no means free from domination. If he wants to utter revolt, he has only the available discursive means, wherein there is only compliance. All he can do is write out his compliance in the form of a mockery, or rather to expose his text to its own mockery, by which the estimable public face of the memo is seen as a disguise for its own hapless comedy.

High Flying at Low Levels

Hierarchy, Composition, and Teaching

> It was with my wonderful students at Texas
> that I discovered that I was at my best as a
> classroom teacher—at Iowa I did not know
> myself as anything else in the public domain.
> Since then, all my writing has come out of my
> teaching.
>
> —Gayatri Chakravorty Spivak

Jane Gallop has a recent essay on teaching that begins, unsurprisingly enough, with a student. But the rest of her first paragraph is curious. She mentions how what she was teaching converged, in part, on her just-published book, and then how teaching threatened, in effect, the next book she was trying to get done. Worst of all, she was commuting weekly from Milwaukee to Houston.[1] I begin an account of teaching with Gallop because my own sense of it has always been framed by high flyers.

It is hard to write about teaching because it is not much valued as a subject worth writing about. Admirable are those authors whose introductory pages include grateful acknowledgment to specific classes in which a subject was engaged, challenged, and developed. This is usually given in one sentence, thereby comprehending the classroom in terms of research, not teaching.[2] If, on the other hand, the majority of your teaching has been, as mine has, freshman composition sections, sophomore introduction-to-literature courses, or junior-level surveys, you will not be generating books. Indeed, you may well have so many themes, examinations, and papers to read that you won't have much time to read books. If you desire to write about what you do anyway, teaching becomes a kind of writing in disguise.

How to represent the experience of teaching classes neither designed nor performed in order to produce texts? A few years ago I was teaching an especially dreary introductory course. Having long ago scrapped the requisite use of hefty anthologies, I had resolved to make do instead with novels—the more off-the-syllabus, not to say off-the-wall, the better. My choices this particular semester had proved to be a disaster. It showed on the midterm. I felt unusually uncomfortable with my distance from the students as I read their examinations, and, once I finished them, wrote a short essay, "Grading the Midterm," about all that a professor cannot say to a class when it is time for a test to be given, and then given back.

I could not get the essay published.[3] Perhaps it was not much good, although I suspect the very subject is just too mundane. Apart from a narrative of eager students and stimulating colleagues, teaching is culturally mandated to do with themes of the big cognitive picture. Teaching is one of those activities about which it is probably good not to have too many thoughts, unless they have to do with the ceaseless need for something *new*: perspectives, connections, pedagogies, anything. Nobody, it seems, wants to hear about the same old routines: calling the roll, keeping office hours, strolling around the room as you lecture. "Whatever pieties to the contrary," states Evan Watkins, speaking of the venerable "binary opposition" between writing for publication and teaching, "publication is always the privileged term, because it names the power of producing 'the new.'"[4]

This privilege is so utterly the case that when luminaries strive to get close to their teaching, they can only approach at all by means of their writing. Hence, at the end of his recent memoir, when Frank Lentricchia at last brings himself to face his upcoming courses, he fancies including a beloved quotation from Kafka as an exam question, and then imagines the following response of two "sleepers" who identify who wrote the words: "You did, you shithead. You wrote everything in this course. That's why we slept. Finish your book on modernism before it's too late."[5] Alas, from the perspective of scholarly production, it is always too late for the classroom.

What status, then, would writing about the commonplaces of teaching have? Much about teaching, in fact, seems as irrelevant to the high road of the public domain as to the research route. In the discourse of this domain, as James Scott has stated, "the effects of power relations are most manifest, and any analysis based exclusively on the public transcript is likely to conclude that subordinate groups endorse the terms of their subordination and are willing, even enthusiastic, partners in that subordination."[6] Therefore, what is acceptable for teachers to say is that they like to teach, and hope to do it better. But many teach in far less enthusiastic and more complicated ways, especially because so much of what they do is held in such low discursive esteem that it effectively ceases to exist.

Moreover, what if a teacher's peculiar striving takes the form of writing? Teachers as a social class do not constitute a subordinate group. But considered in the narrower professional terms of Scott's critique, the work they do in their classrooms is not only subordinate in general to the act of writing but unremarked upon in specific terms by the larger society. The public transcript requires simply that a teacher be dedicated, not detailed. Teaching appears as one of the great selfless examples of human endeavor.[7] In a recent piece on how to have a scholarly career, Dean Whitla mentions individuals such as John Munro, once dean of Harvard College, who left to teach at two Black colleges. Asked once if it is really true that he would come to campus to help any student, Munro is quoted as replying: "Of course—it's no big deal. I just live down the road a couple of miles. If someone calls at 3:00 in the morning, I just hop in my car and just buzz down, no problem."[8]

Munro, presumably, would not be up writing at that hour. Let me set aside my own teaching for a moment. How can the same name be given to what he does and what Gallop does? Although each person is accountable to his or her respective institution in terms of regularly scheduled classroom hours, the work itself seems fundamentally different. Gallop's teaching enables her to conduct research. This is why she can write as follows: "The only language I can summon to describe a powerful experience of doing exactly what I imagine to be good teaching seems bankrupt."[9] Her research aims are not only embarrassed before this language (far better suited for someone like Munro), but they explain why she can ground her essay in discovery of how an erotic relation with students is "knotted" to a professional one.

Munro, on the other hand, would not, I think, express such surprise. His teaching might not be an erotic investment, but it certainly enables him to partake in what the "bankrupt" language Gallop disdains might characterize as "a labor of love." Driving a couple of miles down the road in the middle of a night to help a student testifies just as much to the profoundly social logic of Munro's labor as Gallop's flying a couple of thousand miles once a week does to her own endeavor, which is harder to characterize in social terms at all. It is not rooted in one place. Much of what Gallop does takes place all alone up in the clouds.

Although I have myself taught in four other countries besides the United States, all my teaching has taken place on the ground. But I think I would distinguish myself from Munro through being vexed by the presence of related activity overhead. Munro, most likely, does not care, and he probably sleeps better for it, even during those nights when he gets a student phone call. The public transcript honors his example as a teacher. What Munro does exists to be enacted rather than written. His audience, year after year, presumably consists of grateful students, who are, as the usual discourse goes, "their own reward." If, on the contrary, you want to write about what you do if students are not always grateful and seldom their own reward, does this necessarily mean you seek a different audience, or another kind of reward?

It seems so. The very act of writing about the classroom is for a teacher an incipiently alienating activity. The public transcript does not require it. The research project does not honor it. Therefore, if, according to the public transcript, a teacher is someone who calls the roll dutifully and grades the midterm unproblematically, on what basis is one to articulate a more vexed relationship to these tasks? Moreover, if your classes have been mostly too elementary to be recreated in terms of research, how to avoid the accusation that what you've been doing all these years is staring at the heavens, if you want to maintain instead that some account of your teaching has its own discursive contribution to make?

Teaching for me has meant finding a way to write about it. One reason is that I've had to be so downcast over one particular course, which I want to discuss in the next section of this chapter. The other reason is more complicated. It took the experience of teaching abroad to make me fully realize why until that time I had never been able to make writing about teaching simply emerge as part of doing it. Two things were almost immediately apparent to me during my first year abroad, in Saudi Arabia: I taught better than I did back home, and the customary framework for my activity as a teacher at Clarion State College (as it was known then) was gone. After a couple of months I began to write—about Saudi Arabia, about travel writing. It was as if I had fallen off the professional map. But how could this be?

Once during that year the Saudi chairman called me into his office. He was rifling through some list of American universities that the kingdom had compiled. Clarion, alas, was not on it. "Are you certain you teach at a university?" he asked me. By then I was not even offended. The man was absurd, the whole university (which changed its name halfway through the year) had become a playpen. The students were wonderfully charming, and my Western colleagues enormously stimulating. Each day we all spent hours in the courtyard, drinking tea and exchanging stories, gossip, and ideas. Although we all agreed (after students left) that Saudi Arabia was the most horrible country on earth, we were having a great time. It scarcely seemed to matter where we had come from or what had brought us together.

No institutional space we had variously occupied prepared any of us for Saudi Arabia. To me, King Saud University came to represent the absence of structure, and the rebirth of teaching as a profoundly social experience, embracing students and colleagues both. My teaching was not defined by the mere confines of the classroom. Yet teaching felt complete in itself. I had more desire to reenact before others the comic dialogues and the hapless lessons (for what transpired in the classroom was not very successful) than to represent them somehow in writing. Far more strangely to me, how could writing suddenly appear dispensable—just at the moment when I was in fact writing more than I had since completing my dissertation? To answer this question, I had to try to reconstruct my whole teaching career right up to this most foreign point in time, beginning with the one course that repeatedly depleted all my words.

A long time ago, at a session of an otherwise forgettable conference, one of the participants said something unforgettable about teaching. Every class we teach, she said, is an example of something complete in itself. The semester eventually ends, and with it all our classes. The peculiar dynamic comprising the students grouped in each one will never exist in the same way again. I often think about these words, never with sadness, as I stand before the class the final time for every semester's two sections of composition.

This course comprises half my teaching load. If my teaching experience could be considered quantifiable, exactly half of it would consist of composition, and, since I dislike teaching the subject so much, all of the experience would be sour. The problem finally is not the students, although the range of attitudes and thoughts demonstrable on the part of year after year of eighteen-year-olds is not, to put it kindly, inexhaustible. With good reason do the composition teachers in a recent academic novel by Edward Allen get together to establish a pool, with the prize going to the one who comes closest to guessing the total number of essays submitted to the department entitled, "Abortion: Auschwitz USA."[10]

The problem for me is the writing itself. It is awful. More to my point here, however, is that the writing is inescapable. Eve Kosofsky Sedgwick has an essay partly on her experience teaching a gay and lesbian studies class. "The level of accumulated urgency, the immediacy of the demand that students bring [to such courses] is jolting," she writes. There is one "controversial thing": the course remains a literature course, and therefore "the path to every issue we discussed simply had to take the arduous defile through textual interpretation."[11] Nothing could be more in contrast to composition, where texts are the very point of the course—even if, in the present pedagogical moment whereby students compose through a succession of drafts, production and interpretation keep bumping into each other.

If there are teachers of composition who manage to be jolted by their students as Sedgwick is, I don't know what to reply, except to wonder how they manage to negotiate past the "defile" that even Sedgwick (apparently) can't ignore. What probably happens is this: the defile is transformed into a social relation, through conferences of various kinds. Indeed, to deem the writing that students produce in composition to be part of who they are as human beings or citizens of a community is the key to teaching the course. The crucial thing is that composition be understood not so much as the production of texts but the expression of selves, in a kind of democratic communion with each other, which it is the job of the teacher to encourage and foster.

Consider the following selection of questions "we need to ask ourselves," according to Pam Annas:

> Do we allow students to write about topics that passionately interest them, and are grounded in who they are, in all their multifaceted variety? Do we let them 'play' with free writing, journals, and papers written in the first person but retain as our end of semester goal mastery of the standard objective research paper in the standard format?
> ... How can we invite each student to write out of how and who he or she

is while at the same time equipping each one with the survival skills she or he will need? Do we provide a classroom that is cooperative, a writing community where students learn in part by teaching each other, or do we hang on to authority and the keys to what the right way is?[12]

Compare this description of composition with another from Laura Weaver, in the same collection of articles. The writer is characterizing a particularly difficult semester, in which she taught four courses, including a literature-composition course and two composition courses.

> I counted the number of papers: in addition to numerous smaller papers, I graded rough drafts and final versions of thirty-eight ten-page research papers in a research and report writing class (total—760 pages); rough drafts and final versions of nineteen ten-page research papers in a world cultures class (total—380 pages); and sixty-four three-page papers in a world literature class (total—192 pages). Also, during the same semester in my regular conferences with approximately sixty students I needed to cultivate a smile and a strategy for expressing interest in each student's work.[13]

What to say? Finally these two visions of what it is to teach writing are irreconcilable. One is centered on students, the other on texts. One sees a community, while the other sees a course. In one, the goal is to teach values, while in the other the object is to provide grades. Given this polarization, the particularly interesting thing to me is that by the end Weaver has assumed the terms of the same social relation with which Annas begins. It's very difficult to teach composition and not express interest in each student's work as a manifestation of expressing interest in each student. In a sense, you have to. If the work isn't very interesting, at least the students can be, or have to be.

But once you see through the work to make contact with the students, what happens to the work? It is not clear to me how much Annas needs the mediation of writing at all. I have had plenty of students in composition whose writing became most significantly readable to me as individual expressions of sheer selfhood. I liked them. But then how to judge their themes—especially in a course in which I begin and end by stressing that I grade a paper, not a person? Eventually I had to acknowledge this contradiction as inescapable and irreconcilable. Many teachers of composition, and only composition, especially part-time, temporary ones, probably have to make a career out of resisting the same contradiction. What I did myself was to change the way I taught writing. Out for good went individual conferences. In came "peer editing," a pedagogy primarily useful to me as a means of diffusing and displacing evaluation. Now the remorseless *text* is lodged, permanently for me, I suspect, at the mute center of everything I do in the composition course, which is mainly to read as few themes as possible.

Anything else I previously did—ranging from semesters in which I assigned a theme a week to semesters in which I made absolutely no assignments at all—seems to me now to represent so many attempts to dislodge from the center the necessity of having to read this text. The years in which I made no assignments were my favorite ones. I got to know lots of students, and their writing scarcely got in the way. I trusted one student enough to rent him my house during a year I taught abroad. But alas, you can let students play as much as you want, and regard them as so multifaceted it's a shame they have to punctuate at all. You are still going to have to read what they write before the end of the semester, and make some fateful evaluation that casts aside the human relation you have carefully tried to nurture with as many students as possible, as if each one certified a virtual credential necessary for you to teach the course.

Having to provide a grade is so painfully obvious a mandate—not to say, the mandate—for composition that it took me years to realize how it shaped the worst personal consequence of having to read freshman themes: their corrosive effect on my own writing. I thought I just hated consuming these themes. I am not sure when I became aware how utterly they were affecting anything I wanted to produce myself. Anything. A writer I came to know, who tried to teach composition for the steady income, had to quit, he told me, when he just could not write anymore, not even on those days when he didn't have to teach, much less read themes.

I remember the day when he came into my office with a cartoon about a psychiatrist sitting in a chair with his hand on a lever. He was pulling it, and a patient on a couch was sliding through a hole in the floor. "You're too fucked up—" the caption read, "Next patient, please." We laughed. Unlike my friend, though, I remain to try to understand exactly why. It's important to emphasize how reading freshman themes is so unlike reading any other kind of student writing—or any writing. I like to read term papers in literature courses. I enjoy reading seminar papers for graduate courses even more. I love to read and detail responses to writing of almost any sort. But composition themes act to enlist the teacher in an unusually intimate way with the necessity of evaluation, from the position of a writer as well as a reader.

Some of the reason has to do with the fact that the subjects for the course are either so contrived (see abortion, above) or so personal (as Annas enjoins). The first time I taught a section of composition, over twenty-five years ago as a teaching assistant, the textbook was on modern satire. The writing assignments had to do with literary analysis. But the composition syllabus has been severed from its subordination to that of the literary one for decades now, and composition studies has become a field of inquiry unto itself. Whatever the ideological explanations or professional justifications for these developments, they have emptied out the content of the course for me.[14] Granted, it never had much anyway. One of my oldest friends was once a student in one of my first composition courses. A while ago he got out his old notes, and had us both in stitches at some of my assignments: the pleasures of well-done meat, or the feminine foot as a sexual object. He said I was serious. I cannot believe I was.

Maybe at the very outset I was trying to distance myself from the writing, by making its content resemble that of the venerable "literary" essay. Now I think I understand more clearly why I may have instinctively moved away. Reading the themes (only fifty, rather than closer to sixty, for the two sections in those days) required so much involvement that I seemed to be doing the writing myself. Lisa Ede has a fine description of the process. "My reading of their essays," she states of her composition students, "is, in a sense, contaminated with or directed by the writing I will do in response, even before I begin writing. In responding, I in a sense appropriate my students' texts with my comments, so that when I read a revision I am reading to see how *we* have done."[15] Ede goes on to mention a degree of personal implication so total that, when a student fails, it is as if she fails as well. The imperative to comprehend these themes under the sign of evaluation is so powerful that Ede refers to "reading" them as "grading" them, even though it's been at least ten years since she used individual letter grades.

What about the relation between such reading and her own writing? Ede sensibly concludes that the one feels more like the other (a common self-consciousness and so on), but then goes nowhere with the realization. One explanation immediately suggests itself: she already has gone somewhere, in the writing of the essay itself. Ede, who administers the Writing Lab at her university, conceives of her project within the context of composition studies. That is, in sharp contrast to the way I've taken teaching the subject for most of my career, the composition classroom provides a *research opportunity* for Ede akin, let's say, to the literature classroom of Jane Gallop.

To claim that composition is a respectable discipline is to say that it possesses its own proper authority for "producing the new." Lisa Ede herself may be, for all one knows, a teacher very much like John Munro. But there is now a difference: on one of those nights when a desperate student calls, she might well be up writing. It won't be about literature. Teachers such as me, whose whole professional orientation since graduate school has been literary in nature, now find themselves forced to confront the wholesale reconceptualization of a course that once meant the very antithesis of anything having to do with research or publication. The field of composition has been strong enough for some years to have launched its own high flyers, and I don't think anybody can teach comp anymore without at least occasionally looking up.[16]

So far, alas, the results of my own observation have led me in the wrong direction: to a renewed interest in trying to reconceive the literature classroom, for many of the utopian reasons someone such as Annas counsels us to organize the writing classroom. Students can be instructed to write out in journals their questions or responses to stories read, or to form groups in class in order to have micro-discussions of larger issues in novels. How much do such reconfigurations finally matter to them? I don't know. They matter to me. I suspect they matter to me in inverse proportion to how little even rearranging the chairs (forget about "reconstituting community") matters anymore, when what has to be located is a sentence fragment or a thesis statement rather than a racial assumption or a queer absence.

So what am I doing anymore in the composition classroom, aside from earning a living? I've learned the public transcript if anybody asks: more writing-community-than-thou. Offstage, I've learned a few jokes, especially a lovely old Henny Youngman one about the man who comes home early from work one afternoon. There is a cigar smoking from an ashtray in the living room. His wife protests surprise. She knows nothing. The husband is mad with suspicion. He looks everywhere in the house. Finally he gets to the bedroom. When he opens the closet door, there stands another man, completely naked. "What are you doing here?" thunders the husband. "I don't know," answers the man. "Everybody has to be somewhere."

There is an impassioned moment in the Sedgwick essay cited earlier when she considers the *ressentiment* (her Nietzschean spelling and italics) against the academy in the United States today. In comparison to many other kinds of workers, she states, "academic faculty, in our decentered institutions . . . have had, it seems, more inertial resistance to offer against the wholesale reorientation of our work practices around the abstractions of profit and the market." Sedgwick continues, "For some faculty at some colleges and universities, it is still strikingly true that our labor is divided up by task orientation (we may work on the book till it's done, explain to the student till she understands) rather than by a draconian time discipline."[17]

Undoubtedly Sedgwick is correct in her judgment. But the agenda she describes, and defends, is as much a matter of institutional hierarchy as it is work. "Some" institutions (it almost seems indiscreet to mention that Sedgwick teaches at Duke) purchase their privilege at the expense of others. Gerald Graff states a truth that no one who considers teaching can afford to forget: "How well one can teach depends not just on individual virtuosity but on the possibilities and limits imposed by the structure in which one works."[18] Yet Graff's very own structure precludes him from realizing how most institutions are not so happily "decentered" as Duke or Northwestern, and therefore lack cultural and professional coin. Take the extent to which the polarity of task vs. time can be restated as one of writing vs. teaching. "In fact, some academics see their own writing as a reward for the drudgery of teaching," remarks Valerie Miner.[19] Although Sedgwick herself is careful not to see it this way, she appears to be at least more aware than Graff that ultimately freedom from the draconian capitalist clock is measured by the book rather than the student.

And if she is not aware, somebody who has many more students is. The sheer amount of the clock time in my own very American experience, where I thought I was overworked and unwritten merely because I taught four classes, including two sections of composition, every semester, was rebuked when I began to teach abroad. The example of Brazil is the most instructive I know. Brazilian professors teach at a bewildering array of high schools, language schools, state colleges and federal universities, usually in some combination. Even people at the most prestigious and best-paying federal universities typically have at least one other position somewhere.

Everyone needs to do it for the money. I have a former student in Rio de Janeiro who spends his entire working week, including Saturday, driving to and from two small colleges—one three hours away from the city—as well as a high school. The last time I saw him, he was hard put to compute for me precisely how many classroom hours he worked just to get by—over forty, at any rate. Such a schedule is not uncommon. I know a woman in the south of Brazil who works fifty hours a week at a college and two high schools. Ten of these hours are in administration at the college. This woman's former teacher is a demon of energy widely celebrated for working even more.

One thing, at least, happens to an American who comes to teach in such conditions: his national discourse about whether or not teaching is work is forever circumscribed. "One of the big differences between academics and almost everybody else in society," remarks Lillian Robinson, "is the way we use that word 'work.'"[20] She means of course that teaching is devalued in favor of something more rigorously intellectual and even more distinctively academic, like writing. But in Brazil teaching is not devalued in this way. Academics work like everybody else. Not only do many work in high schools as well. Virtually everybody works in institutions that lack both the material resources and the cultural license for Sedgwick's "inertial resistance."

In the same collection of essays with Robinson, Michelle Tokarczyk writes bitterly of her first postdoctoral job, in which she not only taught business communication and Western literature but joined the Composition Committee. After the non-renewal of her one-year appointment, she writes, "I realized I was viewed as a worker, someone like a domestic, brought in to perform tasks necessary to the family's maintenance, but never counted as part of the family."[21] But in a society that employs domestic workers on a large scale the comparison won't function the same way, not even for temporary or part-time teachers in the United States, although I do not mean to slight those who work three or more jobs and spend many hours each day merely commuting. Brazilian professors (from a U.S. perspective, anyway) work so much to secure an income level that enables them to distinguish themselves from maids that they have no time to align themselves with professors from the very few institutions that operate at some distance from the market economy.

In Brazil my own professional distance from the local professors among whom I taught soon fell away. There was no discursive framework (apart from my being a native speaker of English) to support how my difference could be clearly situated. That is, there was no institutional framework. No matter that I was paid much more (I had a Fulbright) and worked much less. My university meant nothing in Brazil, just as no Brazilian university meant anything in America. The peculiar hierarchy within which any one institution is embedded in its own country simply cannot be mapped onto another country. What this meant was, in effect, and Tokarczyk to the contrary, that I could view myself quite contentedly as a *worker*.

Brazil (blessedly) is not Saudi Arabia. And yet the Federal University of Rio de Janeiro is a much larger, more remote, and thankless institution than King Saud University. Nonetheless, what being a worker meant for me was having available in Brazil new versions of sociality among colleagues and students quite different from those in the United States. Sometimes this was no more profound than students calling professors by their first names. Of course, once more, social relations had to do with cultural differences between the respective countries. I vividly remember the day I was trying to explain Puritan theology in a survey of American literature while the students were bouncing in their seats to the music of a little samba band that had been assembled down the hallway. But the decisive difference in my whole felt experience can be stated bluntly: the absence of the framework supported by universities such as those Sedgwick celebrates, where faculty enjoy another kind of labor because they're free to write.

As Watkins maintains, publication as "original research" continues to determine "the upper levels of status and prestige" in American higher education, as performed by "a tiny percentage of the university-trained workforce in English throughout the country."[22] This is true in Brazil as well, but not in the same way as it is in the United States. Brazilian universities have no common databases or intercollegiate athletic competitions. There is no infrastructural connection among them comparable to American universities. One result is that faculty research does not matter so much. Teaching appears to matter much more—and not merely because, by American standards, there is so much more to do.

I taught better in Brazil because I relaxed into doing it on its own terms. That is, teaching was not contaminated by the sway of a research agenda, which either fell away (original research being almost impossible to do in another country unless it has to do with that country) or abided in some separate realm, like home itself.[23] Of course I could conclude that I just did more varied teaching—including a graduate class that met mostly in an office of the American Consulate one semester because there were two long strikes on campus. I believe I taught better, though, because the teaching itself had the immediacy of a social relation whose professional status had baffled me back home when I could not decide whether I should be writing about teaching, or writing about something entirely removed from teaching.

And yet it was more complicated than this, because in some respects the essence of the social relation had directly to do with writing. In Brazil, as well as Egypt earlier and China a few years before that, the students did the writing, while I supervised. In Brazil and Egypt, in addition to lecturing classes, I supervised M.A. theses. One of my Egyptian students, an army officer, remarked to a colleague that he'd been hearing about scholars all his life, but had never felt he'd met one until me. Scholarly? I was just being friendly. One of my Brazilian students, an excellent cook, made lunch every other week for a few months and then we went over the writing she had done. Each time it felt more like making a social call than having a conference.

Teaching at a provincial university in China was such an engrossing experience that, one semester, teaching a course that came dangerously close to resembling composition proved to be suspiciously close to being fun. The written English of the students was not much worse than those I taught back home. More surprising was that either their sentiments were more sincere or else the exquisite cultural traditions alive in many of them, poor as they were, enabled an astonishingly supple rhetoric of sincerity. Though there were too many students in the class, and though some only opened up, if at all, after class, I read their writing with so much interest that I could only think of what I would write about it. For once, I wanted to write as an extension of my responsiveness, and not as a replacement for a responsiveness I lacked.

The different relation to writing I have enjoyed through foreign students, as well as the different relation to students through writing, climaxed during the second semester of the year at a provincial university in China. I was given the task of supervising the theses of the entire fourth level, or senior class. Each had to write an acceptable thesis to graduate.

For nearly two months, from as early as 7:30 A.M. to as late as 11 P.M., some seventy students besieged me about every conceivable aspect of their writing, from which books would be suitable to choose to what commas each should put in the next draft. What I did must be described as teaching. But the actual experience partook of so many different kinds of activity that I was left with a whole series of individual relationships, many quite personal. There was one student who gradually became aware of how the political critique in Arthur Koestler's *Darkness at Noon* could be applicable to his own country, another who never quite understood the relation between rape and racial prejudice in Erskine Caldwell's *Trouble in July*, and a third whose effusions on Sherwood Anderson's *Winesburg, Ohio* kept resulting in such howlers as "he quenched her thirsty womb."

I wrote a long letter to a friend about the experience of feeling overcome by all these students. If I had not made a copy, and therefore could no longer remember having once read a paper on *Silas Marner* while keeled over on the floor because my back was so sore, I would probably sentimentalize more than I do the most remarkable, depleting thing I have ever done as a teacher. Or perhaps without a copy of the letter I would not be able to connect the supervision with the occasion, some two and a half years later in Egypt, when my lectures on a single novel, Edith Wharton's *House of Mirth*, eventually had to be relocated to an auditorium because so many students had crowded into the small classroom. Striding around onstage like a Shakespearean actor delivering long monologues, I proceeded to spin out lavish summaries of the plot to an audience who had swelled to upwards of five hundred. Afterwards, in a courtyard, I would chat to groups of them: what Americans thought about sex, what Egyptians thought about Israel, and so on. Every so often somebody would mention one of the characters in Wharton's novel. It always seemed to me we were talking about real people.

Back home, in between the years in China and Egypt, I wrote an article not so much about teaching English in China as about the political stakes of the very fact of Chinese learning the language. Two years later it was lost in a box of books that never reached me in Egypt. The piece was more or less scholarly in nature—that is, too academic for *Harper's* and not enough so for *College English*, each of which was forthcoming with a requisite rejection letter. I often think about this article now. Its problem was, I suppose, either that I could not break sufficiently away from my actual experience of having taught, or else that I failed to use this experience as the exclusive basis for raising larger social and political questions. Maybe, though, there was a deeper failure. Why had I not made an extra copy? Did I somehow desire my words to be lost? Although I did eventually publish a few articles of a more general nature on living abroad, this essay on English in China is the only writing I ever tried to do in any way related to teaching in a foreign country. It seems to me now entirely apt that the text eventually wound up at some entirely unknowable spot on earth. Maybe it's still in the country's dead letter office.

"There is no fixed place that we inhabit," concludes James Phelan in his account of fifteen months of his professional life. "Instead, we live in a place — or better, many places — that are constantly changing, and our relations to those places also change as our experiences draw upon or develop different parts of ourselves."[24] These words make strange reading for me. Phelan begins his account of teaching by mentioning that he has spent ten years living in the same physical place. I end my account considering how a few years teaching abroad have not very much changed my relation to the same place I have lived for twenty-five years. Abroad, there were always students who needed something: better spoken English, more refined skills in reading, wider knowledge of the world. Back home, on the other hand, it is no more clear than it ever was what students need — except at the lowest level, that is, composition, where the need for improved job skills or positive work attitudes seems to me at once more crucial and less specific to higher education than it has ever been in my career.

Such drastically different scenes of national instruction, in turn, only exacerbate anew my need for some relation to students mediated through writing. This need continues to be quite personal — located for me as "personal" by my disciplinary circumstances as well as my institutional ones. If the writing should take the form of research, the classes take up too much time and fail to provide scholarly provocation. If, instead, the writing could be something else, I've never quite discovered what. In either case, the pleasures of teaching as a social activity feel to me uneven, sporadic, ephemeral — and unwritten, if not unwritable. I don't know how to disguise them.

Meanwhile, up above, the theoretical pleasures of teaching are celebrated as never before. Consider, for example, Daniel O'Hara on Frank Lentricchia, whose "psychic agency" is found to be "a radically ambivalent dialectic of self-overcoming identification and critical differentiation, loving transference and defensive distantiation." There is more. Lentricchia, according to O'Hara, has at his source "the ancient classical model of self-development derived from the complex ever-changing relationship of the pedagogic pair of mentor and student with their (at least) latently erotic bond."[25] Does this mean that Lentricchia is in love with himself, or rather the student-in-himself?

I do not think it means that O'Hara is bidding us to care whether Lentricchia puts Kafka on the exam in his course on modernism, or even whether he gives an exam. Come to this, O'Hara (or we) may not care whether Lentricchia gives the course. The sort of "dialectic" O'Hara represents is ultimately, I think, beyond teaching. Furthermore, it is beyond teaching because it is so comfortably, or inescapably, within the confines of writing. I may compare my old incredulity at teachers who state they are content to do all their writing in student journals. How can they communicate everything to their students? There has always seemed to me something *more* to say, even in a student journal. But in Lentricchia's "model" there is so much more that students only get in the way. If it is always possible to stop teaching in ways you cannot stop writing, it is even easier to keep writing in ways you cannot begin teaching.

I do not believe I ever dreamed of writing so radically. As it is, I still never want the best classes to stop, not even two-and-a-half-hour graduate seminars. I might be a better, or at least more dedicated, teacher than I have made myself out to be. I may have always enjoyed teaching more than I have been capable of reflecting upon, for it does not take any teacher long to learn that teaching cannot be defined in terms of his or her best classes. Nonetheless, the trouble has remained the same: writing opens up the space of teaching. If you do not discover a book there (or at least an article or two), it is hard to be content with whatever you do in the classroom.

Especially in a profession where, far above, many flights continue without students on board. Indeed, the planes are better and bigger than ever. (Once we set aside cheap commuter flights, full of students and part-time, temporary instructors.) Despite troublesome questions about the availability of funding and the significance of the whole mission, there appears to be room for more diverse people on board now. But all tickets do not cost the same, and some destinations do not result in everybody doing the same thing once the plane lands, not even on the international routes. Although

I managed to touch down in distant places where I have done some of my best teaching, I mostly worked with teachers who had never flown and never worried that they ought to try to write about their work. It has been a decade now since I taught among them, and yet I still wonder if I would rather finish my career among colleagues whose position is so fixed that eventually they will just sink into the earth, or among colleagues who try to keep their feet on the ground while noises overhead distort or silence what they say.

Writing Resignation

The Donkey on the Minaret and the President's Papers

Nothing before or since has distinguished my teaching career quite as much as resigning from it. A little more than a decade ago I resigned twice in the same month, from two separate institutions in different countries. In what follows, I want to print both letters of resignation and describe something of their respective, though very related, circumstances. It has been very unusual for some years in academic life, I believe, for a tenured professor to have occasion to write a letter of resignation. Before explaining each of mine, first let me consider why it should be so unusual in the first place.

The simplest reason is tenure itself. As the numbers of part-time or temporary faculty have increased, tenure has become harder to get.[1] The harder it has been to get, the easier it has been to keep—and even overreach. An interesting recent case in point is that of Tzvee Zahavy of the University of Minnesota, a professor of religion for seventeen years. After he had taken another tenured position with the University of North Carolina at Charlotte, only a semester passed before he was discovered. He was then fired by Minnesota and forced to return both salary and moving expenses to North Carolina.

In the course of defending Professor Zahavy's actions, a column in the *Chronicle of Higher Education* written by a friend of his recounts some late outrages at his own university: the professor who refused to teach her course of 350 students because of a fight with the dean, or another professor who refused to have anything to do with his colleagues, not even speaking to them, after a decision not to reappoint him as head of a committee. Anybody who has been teaching at a university anywhere in the United States knows of similar examples. Nothing ever comes of them. They appear on no public transcript.

The author of the *Chronicle* column does not say that tenure now forgives all sins. What he states is this: "We professors have very cushy jobs — if that is how we want things."[2] Whether or not "we" want "things" this way (as if they were merely a function of our desire), there has been one consequence: just as there is virtually no cause any longer that merits firing (setting aside the volatile subject of sexual harassment), there is none that merits resigning. Perhaps part-time people more regularly resign. But then they do not enjoy the "cushy" conditions of tenure so unfortunately extended by Professor Zahavy.

Widely published professors at major research institutions might also write letters of resignation. The same column mentions an instance involving "top" professors at Brown University resigning together. But such people enjoy even more job mobility than poor Professor Zahavy, who might have had enough clout himself not to try to have it both, or rather two, ways. Top people, unlike part-timers, simply receive offers, decide where to go, and move. "Sitting in a Japanese tea room off the rue du Faubourg St. Honoré," Cathy Davidson writes in a recent memoir of a visit with her husband to Paris, "we found ourselves thinking about the various jobs we'd been offered and suddenly knew that we wanted to take the positions at Duke University, situated in the lush, overly green Carolina countryside that reminded us of rural Japan."[3]

But what if, when you go, the only way is out of the profession entirely? The corporatist policies of the contemporary university virtually mandate a new Ph.D. to consider just such an exit while trying at the same time to gain a tenure-track point of entry. Before century's end, we can expect to hear more stories than we have at present from the first generation of aspiring professors tensed, not to say trained, to *expect* widespread permanent unemployment — stories, that is, not about their inclusion but their exclusion. If so, my guess is that these stories will not be "personal," a "mode" that, as Charles Altieri writes, "remains quite thin as a stance for . . . making substantial cultural claims—unless the critic goes on to develop a theoretical case in which the personal works primarily as a representative example, offered as a means of extending knowledge rather than a means of fostering intimate relations with some community."[4] The problem, I think, will not be so much the lack of knowledge as the lack of relation. People who leave the profession represent a logic of exit too uncomfortably intimate with (if not inseparable from) the logic of entrance and endurance. In this respect, it ultimately comes to much the same thing for the "community" whether you have been part of it too long as a professor or have never managed to be part of it at all after graduate school.

The profession of English was undoubtedly a more permanent one twenty years ago, when *College English* published a short article by Samuel Pickering, Jr., entitled "Good-bye Dartmouth, or Thirty-Five, Fat, Slow, and Unemployed." The change in the profession since that time could be indicated merely by the unlikelihood today of one of the discipline's leading journals publishing such an "occasional" piece, which disdains making a "theoretical case." Pickering, it seems, was fired, and he has nothing much to conclude about it, except that he was a bit of a "maverick," went to the right schools, feels consoled that he's a Southerner, will miss Dartmouth forever, and has already applied to a couple of places.

Only his style discloses, I think, a despair Pickering can't write away. For example, he writes as follows about a possible business career: "Even if the right offer glided into my mailbox, there is not enough backfat hanging in the larder for me to peacock up for Madison Avenue, not even enough for me to rooster along Church Street in Nashville."[5] I suppose figurative feats are necessary in order to try to avoid—at least in public— the almost inescapable self-pity attendant upon losing a job. Today, on the other hand, the almost irrepressible self-aggrandizement attendant upon having a job is the customary note, especially if you are in danger neither of being fired nor of having to write a letter of resignation if you want to move.[6]

How to write a letter of resignation, and what might be signified beyond the personal in so much as contemplating one? Advising new Ph.D.s with respect to the current historical moment, Paula Caplan states at one point: "Have an exit path, an idea of what you can do if you leave your present institution or academia altogether, to help alleviate any feeling of being trapped and totally dependent upon your personal setting."[7] But Caplan includes no advice on when to write a letter of resignation, or how. Neither does Altieri, and yet my sense is that such a letter is rather necessarily implicated in what he terms autobiographical criticism providing, as a mode of expression, "the kind of texture, detail, immediacy, sense of idiosyncratic difference necessary to extend contemporary culture's struggles against the hegemony of universals, or the hegemony of its apparently more modest brother, the quest for the representative."[8]

Does one necessarily resign *on some basis?* And if one writes it out, and wants the writing to be important, is the basis necessarily going to test the limits of the personal, either sinking beneath its own weight or stiffening against some weightier hegemony? Composing my own two letters, I recall now the vivid sense of attempting to make a public statement of some sort—even if nobody else would ever read what I wrote. Considered as "transcripts," each letter, no matter how different from the other, felt oddly private and public at the same time. To this day, I have never read another letter of resignation. How different is their rhetorical warrant either among themselves, or from (say) private letters of protest written to public officials because of some felt wrong or injustice? How undisguised can such letters afford to be about being (as I even more vividly recall my own to be) *fun* to write—as if the sheer act of writing transforms irreconcilable conflicts into play?[9]

I first resigned because the public and private conditions of my employment had not come apart as completely as I had imagined. The public part seemed already gone. My Fulbright award to teach in Saudi Arabia was for one semester. I had signed a private contract with the Saudis for the second semester, and therefore represented the American government no longer. The teaching remained the same. Both its intimacies and follies were as enjoyable as the first semester—up to one fateful announcement during a department meeting. And then not even teaching in Saudi Arabia appeared to me to be so wonderfully free of standards or ambitions. Suddenly, with the mention of a conference, the whole disciplinary *outside* was back like a return of the repressed. I thought I had kept any sort of politics away from my classroom, and safely simplified the kinds of differences permitted inside it. I was even farther away from the profession than I was from the country.

So, soon afterward, I wrote my first letter of resignation. Is it not the sole text it is possible for an academic (and maybe anyone else) to write in which the author enjoys complete authority? It felt so to me because the fateful division between private experience and professional role—so bedeviling off the page as well as on—appeared available momentarily to summon up and represent as a necessary unity. Miraculously, there was the realization: *you* are the center of your letter of resignation, and you comprehend yourself utterly as the creature of dishonored criteria or violated values. I enjoyed writing my letter so much that a couple of weeks later I wrote another one. Of course I forgot that in resignation, as in so much else, the second time winds up being farce.

Eve Sedgwick is far more knowing about the mysteries (if not the uses) of performativity. She lately speaks of how Foucault's critique of repression seems, alas, to have led to "mappings that seem not to have motivated readers to account to themselves for the strictly segregated, paroxystically aesthetic pleasures that at the same time motivate and underpin them."[10] But I had not yet read enough Foucault and I had never heard of Sedgwick. So I presumed myself to be able to write either as I was or in disguise, and, far more important, to be able to tell the difference as well as to trust somebody else to be able to tell the difference. On March 15, 1982 I composed the following letter to my Saudi chair.

Dr. Ali Hejazi
Chairman, Department of English
King Saud University

Dear Dr. Hejazi:

This letter is a statement of my intention to resign from the English department. The most immediate reason has to do with the circumstances arising from the announcement of the Conference on Teaching English to Arab Students, to be held in Jordan next month, though I would like to put forth this reason in a larger context.

First, the Conference. Let me outline the sequence of events:

1. You announce the Conference at a department meeting and request those members interested to write papers.

2. The Faculty Council subsequently meets, and decides that, of the four permitted to attend the Conference, two are selected on the basis of their longer experience teaching Arab students. No basis is ever given out for the other two.

3. You inform me of this decision, and proceed to question the paper I inform you I have written—my experience is too limited.

4. My paper is accepted by the Conference, and the director issues me a formal invitation to attend.

No need to detail the rest of this. I see you. You suggest I see Dr. Alathal, since the Council will not reconsider its decision. Next day it's Dean Jad I'd better see first. I do. Already apprised of my visit to you, he duly sends me on to Dr. Alathal, who, however, has not been apprised by anyone. I now write this letter approximately a week later from my first visit to the Vice-President, who by now has had a chance to speak to everybody and have everybody speak to him. Result: it's "in the best interests of the University" that the Council decision stand.

This is very unfortunate, because it's certainly not in my best interests. Indeed, it's not in any interest of me, or about me. I find myself left with a paper I wrote wholly at your suggestion, which was accepted despite what I might call your wisdom, but which I have been denied the opportunity to read because— well, because an arbitrary category seems to have been devised to exclude me.

I want to be very clear. It's the arbitrariness of this entire process—its secret, makeshift, summary nature—which prompts me to submit this letter. There seems to be nothing in my contract which obligates the University to pay for my expenses to a conference for which I have had a paper accepted. Well and good. But the University is sending people anyway, and by criteria quite different than those originally implied and certainly quite different than those of any other institution of higher learning I have known. Conferences, one assumes, have to do with producing as well as consuming knowledge; this one, one infers, has solely to do with consumption. And consumption, moreover, precisely by those logically less in need of the knowledge—namely, those who have taught Arab students the longest! Insofar as these worthies are conceived of as possibly producing knowledge as well: the Council required nothing demonstrable, and (if I have it correctly) disdains the approved results of anyone who has managed to produce anything.

If this state of affairs is an example of "the best interests of the university," then I am compelled to conclude that these interests are wholly administrative. That is, few administrators want to contravene the decisions of a faculty council. I don't quite know how to characterize, in turn, the interests of this body, except to venture that they are not scholarly. I should have thought at the very least that the Council would have wanted to accord recognition to the scholarly pursuits of its fellows.

But I have had little enough support in any scholarly endeavor I have attempted during some six months at King Saud University. I would be less than candid if I did not say that I write this letter against the background of the Fulbright award which originally brought me here. You will recall (I can't forget) that I was given no opportunity to teach the subject upon which the award was based, much less any other authority, privilege, or responsibility beyond those of a regular contractee. (The one lecture I did give, outside the kingdom, was permitted me only with the charming rationale that I was "not working for the University.") That was last semester. This semester the International Communications Agency has notified the University that the U.S. government has continued my award on an "honorary" basis. But it seems to matter as little when it is not actual as when it was. Some categories the University is not pleased to accord any existence to at all. I regard this matter of the Jordan conference as but another, final example of how utterly any *scope* has been denied me in my still somewhat official presence here.

Enough. I offer my resignation because I see no value in continuing as a member of a faculty which acts in bad faith and consigns to irrelevance the scholarly efforts of its peers. I trust you will have the courtesy to let me know as soon as possible whether or not my resignation is accepted.

Most sincerely,

At the center of this letter, I think, are a number of disguised things. One is how the Saudis treated contractees: with such dismissiveness, contempt, and stupidity that examples never failed to astound the rest of us, mostly Westerners. We loved being astounded and outraged. The Saudis provided an inexhaustible fund of narratives, some of the best I've ever heard in my life. But secretly we hated the fact that we could have no illusions. We were there only for the money. The Saudis could do what they wanted with us. Employment began when we relinquished our passports.

It continued while we swallowed our intelligence. My letter does not make clear that the two people selected "on the basis of their longer experience teaching Arab students" were in fact the two Saudi members of the department. They had not written papers at all. None of the rest of us had heard of such an august body as the "Faculty Council" before. It seemed like just another fiction dreamed up by the Saudis so they could vote themselves more opportunities to leave the country. Perhaps one has to have lived in the kingdom to understand something of the vast collective yearning to leave on the part of everyone, from the richest Royal to the lowest Yemini menial.

My letter does articulate something of how having a Fulbright distinguished me from every other contractee. The invitation to lecture in Egypt that I was able to take advantage of was a source of wonderment to all. But I only touch on the frustrations. My award was to teach American literature, for example. But the department had no courses in this subject. I wound up teaching Flaubert and Dostoevsky. After awhile having a Fulbright meant nothing more than being able to get my mail at the American Consulate and my groceries at an Air Force base.

In effect, the Fulbright made me a *representative* figure. But what I represented was not the Fulbright program, except insofar as this program can be conceived of in purely political terms. The Saudis were happy to have an experienced teacher free for a semester, while the Americans were happy to please the Saudis. Neither side was particularly interested in some wider benefit to be derived from the award. Some such benefit, on the other hand, was the reason I took it to be one of distinction; it is not necessary, after all, to select someone for a Fulbright just so that a department somewhere abroad can have another teacher.

But what is teaching? What can even someone who is a Fulbright Professor do other than meet a regularly scheduled class in a classroom? Reading my letter now, I see I yearned for some *other* to teaching, always so remorselessly conceived of according to textbooks and clocks. I'd never known any terms different from these. I wanted to, desperately. So the desire simmered during the months when, so ironically, I learned to become more content with teaching than I ever had in my life. By the second semester, the Fulbright award represented for me the abandoned name for something other than teaching, more readily abandoned when actually it enabled me to do nothing but teach.

And yet I was not the only one to prove unable to let the award go so easily. When it became known that only four in the department would be permitted to attend the Jordan conference, including two contractees, there was wide agreement that I would be one. "You have a Fulbright, after all," everybody said. But the award represented nothing to the Saudis, and once more I was faced with how futilely it abided as signifying something to me, despite my effort to will whatever this might be away. When the names of the two colleagues chosen became known, I realized I had failed. No matter that the paper I had written was not much good. What mattered was that it represented scholarship of some dim sort. The classroom could be transformed. Teaching could be written.

Perhaps the most significant thing not expressed in my letter is simple outrage at having wasted my time writing something. To each endeavor, of course, its own waste. Even successful teaching involves lots of it: lengthy explanations to students who never get the point, intricate preparations for class that turn out to be unnecessary, and so on. But hours of my teaching at King Saud University, during and after class, were so pleasantly spent on warm, eager, uncomprehending students that by the time I resigned I had almost forgotten how writing represents the opposite of waste to me. Writing is a principle of order. It aims at the preservation of its energies, and aspires to the effacement of its conditions. All you need, as many writers have claimed, is a room of your own. The classroom, in contrast, is someone else's.

Consequently, to hear the initial announcement of the Jordan conference was like being awakened from a dream. Subsequently, I suppose I wrote the letter of resignation to assure myself that I could not go to sleep again, nor permit myself to be lulled back into it. Who did I represent? Ultimately only myself, although at the time I took myself to be representing, aside from the Fulbright program, all my fellow teachers. They wanted to resign just as much as I did (if not for the same reasons), but could not, for motives I tried not to judge. Unlike me, after all, none of them had permanent jobs back in their own countries.

"An individual who is affronted may develop a personal fantasy of revenge and confrontation," writes James Scott, "but when the insult is but a variant of affronts suffered systematically by a whole race, class, or strata, then the fantasy can become a collective cultural product."[11] By the time I wrote the letter so many affronts were known to me that it was impossible not to feel that I was articulating the kind of fantasy described here. Indeed, by criticizing the Saudis in print in *any* way I was in effect making public a segment of what Scott terms a "collective hidden transcript." It should not have surprised me that to go public with even a segment would be to discover fantasy as a soberingly different thing from real power relations, in which "hidden" things are absolutely crucial.

The Saudis took a couple of weeks to accept my resignation. I suppose they thought I was simply a fool. So did the Americans at the Consulate. They may have respected my principles more. But they were diplomats who had to think of their own careers, and the language of principles was finally no less alien to them than to the Saudis. As for my fellow contractees back at the University, they were probably as pragmatic as everyone else, except that some manifestation of principle rebuked them more personally. Therefore, I came to feel more like a leper than a moral hero. Soon I stopped going to campus. You teach among a group of people. You resign alone.

And then what do you do? Perhaps you take a trip. I did. Nobody wants to accuse the Saudis of not paying well; the rebuke on campus, particularly to people who taught there only for the money, was that I was casting aside over $10,000 of what remained of my salary by resigning. What the hell, why not a safari in Kenya? Did somebody say dreams? I had plenty of the local money, riyals. I also had more dreams than I was consciously aware of. One thing you probably do not normally do after writing one letter of resignation is write another. Nonetheless, before leaving for Kenya, I did, this time to my own institution back home. The chair of my department was an old friend of sorts. Understanding very little of my own motives, I was sure he would understand.

Dear Fran,

This letter is to announce my intention to resign from the department.

If there are contractual obligations I have, please notify me as soon as possible. I don't believe there are. I write now so that the department will have time to bend its collective will (well, part of the department, anyway, and "will" is one way to describe the part it acts with) to the annual task of selecting a candidate, and then defining the position to suit the candidate. (I just realized I may have the order wrong. Forgive me. I write in some haste and considerable moral anxiety.) I do hope there's time. My time, alas, is over.

I feel I owe you, as well as my colleagues in the department, some explanation. I'll try to be brief.

Last semester I taught one Saed Humdullah Ibn Saud. You guessed it. A member of the royal family. His father is a direct descendent of King Abdulaziz, the son of the former King Saud (the incompetent, dissolute one who died in Cairo, and whom they've lately named the university after).

I passed Saed. Of course I had long ago realized that he, no more than his fellows (some of whom were pleased with me and offered me gifts), could not meet the standards I would normally apply to U.S. students, much less the more exalted standards I of course have grown accustomed to expecting of Clarion students. But his attendance was (excepting the month he flew to Paris) regular, his English was intelligible, his politeness was impeccable. All things considered (my Fulbright, AWACS, cultural pluralism, the plight of the petrodollar, and the oil glut among them) I decided to pass him. I feel I can meet my maker with this knowledge — or his, if it turns out that way.

Saed has two brothers, Ahmed and Abdul. Fine boys. Neither of them called me a *kifer* (roughly "infidel"). I met them one evening when Saed invited me to the palace outside Riyadh for — well, for what our feeble English word, "dinner," simply does not describe. Two young lambs were slaughtered in my honor (as is the custom, I got the greatest delicacy, the eyes — which taste I might describe, sort of like what all the themes written in English 110 would taste like if they could be ground up and condensed into a digestible entity). They were served by sequined Sudanese boys, while we sat around on silk cushions, sipped the most exotic liquid with a tamarind base out of jeweled chalices, nibbled on melons, and told sad stories of the death of things. Of course there were no dancing girls. This was a strict Islamic household and such fantasies are the product of vulgar Western prejudices.

That evening I also met the father, Hisham. "Met," I write, but we didn't talk much. Very reserved, severe man. Looks like the Ayatollah, only stouter.

So imagine my surprise when, a few weeks later, a driver appeared at my door (an American! he used to teach basic writing at three different schools in Philadelphia until one day a student knifed him while they were arguing about a comma splice), and summoned me back to the palace. (Another vulgar Western idea is that all Saudi royals have Rolls-Royces. The car was a modest Porsche.) I was ushered into the paternal presence. Hisham snapped his fingers, and a bottle of scotch appeared as if by magic. He gestured me to it, and, as I gulped my first round, proceeded to present the following proposal.

Saed, it seemed, had developed a considerable admiration for me. My lack of sarcasm, my patience, and my sociability were specifically mentioned. (Well you might ask how he could *know?*) This admiration was enough to commend me to the father, though he continued that he had made inquiries and indeed revealed that he knew my professional record right down to the last Composition Committee I had served on. Only the fact that I had spent so much of my professional life teaching composition seemed to bother him, until I explained the depth not only of my own commitment but that of the Commonwealth of Pennsylvania to the verbal (as distinct from the intellectual — a point Hisham had particular trouble with) well-being of its youth.

The proposal? That I be employed to tutor his two younger sons until college age, and afterwards only by mutual agreement. In all aspects of English and especially English literature. (Dad, it seemed, loved Dickens and had developed a curious enthusiasm for the fiction of Ronald Firbank long ago while a student at the London School of Economics. During that time, incidentally, he learned to loathe the British, whose "epicene civility" he spoke of with great contempt.) Essentially, that was it.

I would only be permitted three months vacation. I would be expected to be available at all times, and to accompany the family on their frequent visits to Geneva, London, and (less frequently) Cairo. Hisham was extremely apologetic when he mentioned that he would only be able to tender me a salary of 180,000 riyals (about $55,000).

However, there would be compensations. A Mercedes 240 would be at my disposal. I would of course have my own living quarters. (I think this is the small villa, the glint of the evening sun off whose blue tile I had seen earlier that night.) All the latest films would be available to my VCR—uncensored (an assurance this wily Arab conveyed with a devious wink so characteristic of the Sauds). A liquor allowance would be permitted me. (Hisham allowed himself to be nothing if not a man of the world, even if not all of it was Islamic—yet.)

He was most concerned about the matter of the modesty of his wives (I don't know how many) and daughters. Since he was a man of liberal views, and since, moreover, I was already a grown man, Hisham declared that there was no need even to entertain the idea I should be castrated. (I gulped a whole glass of scotch at this one.) Though it would not be permitted of me to have a wife ("in matters of the mind I am celibate") I think Hisham was at his most wily, even puckish, when he spoke rather too loftily of how "from time to time certain concessions to the flesh might be arranged, even for a whole weekend." Surely I am wrong to seem to remember him mentioning something about notorious Bangkok in this connection?

Enough. I said I'd try to be brief. I don't have to put down the problems. Let me just wave at one: even though in the next seven or eight years under this scheme I'd earn more than the next twenty-five at Clarion (tax-free of course, and for the entire period, even if Reagan is re-elected and/or lives), *I would lose my tenure.* No need to turn to Emerson. For an academic, what possible Compensation could there be for such a loss?

I really can't bring myself to write here of the emotions evoked in me by the knowledge I'll never evaluate another freshman theme again. (All the new topics I have now! "Snow vs. sand" for comparison-contrast, or "The camel: fact or fiction" for the research paper. It's too sad.) I hope I don't sound too immodest if I do put down at least the fact of the pain it causes me to realize how unique and indispensable my contribution would have been to that meat of the departmental menu, Eng. 170, "The Literary Experience" (assuming the title hasn't been changed again). I have but to think of the hunger for literary theory on the part of Clarion English majors (still in double digits?) and a decision not to return seems like the most heinous betrayal. What—I have had to ponder during these long desert nights—would the department do without me, much less I without it?

This is very painful, and I have had to conclude that, like a married couple who have known each other too well and too bloodlessly, we can part and we must part. Ahmud and Abdul will be the sons I've never had. My destiny is in the East. *Insha'allah* as they say here, "as God wills it." I may have more time to polish up my manuscript on parody, but I don't even care about this, nor whether or not the riyal is stronger than the dollar, or whether the House of Saud is really built on sand. To cite the Arab proverb: "He who takes a donkey to the top of a minaret must also know how to get it down." Maybe it's just that I don't know how to get down.

You're right to sense that I wobble. But I must still ask you to take my name plate from my office door and distribute my dittoes from over a decade among the department. Of my books, please send the *Harbrace Handbook* only. The rest you can just dole out to needy majors, until, by 1990, you can foist what remains onto the last English major.

I do wobble. I miss the rest of the pack. Maybe you should post this on the lounge bulletin board and have them bray at it. Such heights were never meant for donkeydom, and there is the consolation that those for whom my year's absence has seemed too short can graze more easily on their lawns this summer because they will know that to get a Fulbright from Clarion is only to have one's nature changed utterly. Many have conspired to get me up here, and now I can't get down. Perhaps Darrel would like to print this in his journal as a cautionary tale to his readers.

I'll try to stay in touch. Send me a few themes once in awhile and perhaps an especially telling midterm from 170. Meantime I urge that at the first fall department meeting a motion be adopted to the effect that no one ever be permitted to apply for a Fulbright again—anywhere. This will not only insure smooth and sufficient staffing for all the comp sections for the next decade to come. It will also insure that anybody who manages to get out for a year will ever be so foolish as to think he can get back. I fear a life not spent fighting for General Ed requirements will not be life, but I'm

resigned,

c.c.   Whoever is the new Dean
        Dean Still
        President Bond (unless you've got still another new one)

What happened as a result of this letter has a certain local fame in my department. I've never learned all the details. The chair and I proved unable to discuss precisely how he responded to the letter when he first read it. I gather he swallowed it whole, and mentioned my resignation at a meeting he chanced to have soon after. The news spread rapidly, fanned by the glee of the member of the department who especially hated me. Within a day or two, people somehow crowded into my office to get some books from the shelves. Other books were removed and laid out on a table in the coffee lounge.

The same day I wrote the letter of resignation, I wrote to a friend in the department, and referred to the writing as a parody. Was I subconsciously concerned lest the letter be taken seriously? Had this woman not returned from a long weekend, heard what had happened, and told the chair that of course my letter was meant as a joke, I suppose my office would have been sacked by the end of the week. As it was, by the time my friend had spoken to the chair, he had already written a letter to me, expressing his regret that I had resigned and wishing me well.

My first response to *his* letter was to believe it was meant, in turn, as a joke of its own. I tried to recall what I had written. How could anybody believe the lurid story I'd concocted? Or, even if anybody could, how to credit a letter in which I made so many silly or sarcastic references to composition? If the whole department did not know how I felt about teaching this subject, surely my friend did. Didn't he? And how could anybody think I was "sociable?" I read his letter the day I returned from Kenya, in the midst of a little welcome back party. New levels of merriment were reached as everyone learned the story of my resignation.

Within an hour I was able to talk to the chair, and confirm what he had known by then for some days: my letter was not serious. If he felt more foolish in how he had read my letter or in how he had written his own, I could not tell. I was never sure, during the ensuing years, whether he quite accepted the crucial difference I maintained between sharing a joke with him and playing a joke on him. Our relationship was never the same after this episode—unless I now want to comprehend it as never having been the relationship I presumed when I wrote the letter.

Perhaps, whatever it was, I really wanted to destroy my relationship with my own university, as personified in one man. If you do something irrational, there is no end to the logic you can extend to the act once you are in a position to reconstruct its possible motives. Of course the most obvious reason I wrote a parody of a letter of resignation is that I wanted to write a real one. Indeed, I just had. But this first letter took no comparable risks, and only served to disguise the letter of resignation I had really been wanting to write for years about my permanent job.

It has taken me years more to understand precisely why I wanted to resign, and why I would have attempted a certain writing-out of my motives while in, of all places, a foreign country. Of course some of them were local, ephemeral, and personal; it shocks me now, for example, to see how much contempt for a few colleagues I had then. At first I thought these reasons (combined with horror at having to teach comp again) were pretty much all there were. They are not. What having a Fulbright did, in fact, was stage for me a certain realignment of the relationship between private and public experience in my professional life. In effect, I had gotten released time (impossible to secure at my university to this day), in which I was able to see how I could make *use* of both orders of experience by translating each into the other more fully and creatively than I ever could have realized back home.

Back home I never could have discovered my experience in a condition of what has come to be known, a decade later, under the name of "postcoloniality." In Saudi Arabia—at any rate a decade ago—the whole globe was reduced to so many margins of the Arab imperium. A national classification was employed in order to grade levels of work: Koreans as auto mechanics, Egyptians as doctors, and so on. Only the university seemed to destabilize the Saudi system. Our neighbors were from Pakistan, Morocco, Egypt, and South Africa, and you could not determine in which departments they taught on the basis of where they were from. The only constant was that everybody I lived among or met was a diasporic academic. For all I knew there really *were* Americans who once taught comp in Philadelphia now in the employ of sheiks. Everybody's story was vividly individual, yet in ways that only made sense as part of larger patterns of historical or structural dislocation.

Homi Bhabha has an essay in which he suggests at one point that world literature could be considered an "emergent, prefigurative category" not for the venerable theme of each nation's peculiar cultural traditions but for "transnational histories of migrants, the colonized, or political refugees— these border and frontier conditions."[12] In the 1990s, still under the auspices of a Fulbright in American literature, I would probably be more comfortable—not to say fashionable—teaching Flaubert and Dostoevsky. And I would probably be more uncomfortable officially representing a peculiar national cultural tradition, on the one hand, while on the other actually exploring the boundaries of that tradition in a postcolonial space.

Of course people who have Fulbrights do not necessarily take on the character of postcolonials. But they are often automatically inserted into nations where, as in Saudi Arabia, the society is a pure fiction, the authoritative stories are written elsewhere, and everybody is busy trying to write himself or herself either out of one narrative or into another. In such an atmosphere, you become extraordinarily sensitive to how you are being excluded as well as how you are being included. I detested the way I had been included, and so used my postcolonial license in order to write myself out of a crude contractee narrative.

Yet by employing the more elevated national idiom set up by the Fulbright program, I simultaneously wrote myself into another narrative. If postcoloniality teaches anything, I think, it is that you cannot get out of either nations or narratives so easily once you leave home. You remain embedded, often in complicated ways, in affiliations not easy to articulate. Cathy Davidson's travel book about Japan is in one sense a cautionary narrative about how you get out—out of the conditions of your job, out of the country—only to eventually get farther in. Not only does Davidson make a career move to a place because it reminds her of her beloved Japan. She builds a Japanese house there.[13]

But if you cannot literally relocate your professional narrative, and you cannot rewrite it according to the dominant discourse, what to you do if you still want out? One thing you do, I believe, is what I did: you write another, still more hidden, insubordinate transcript. Of course it is haplessly your own and no one else's. You stay repressed. You resist, but with no glamour. You write in disguise. The trouble is, as you are perfectly aware, some disguises remain better than others. Some are so good they do not even seem to be disguises.

Gayatri Spivak has one of the best. A long recent essay is characterized by the editors of the special issue of the magazine in which it appears as "a dazzling series of geographical excursions (from Algeria to Bengal to Singapore to Bangladesh to Italy to Canada)—where our point of entry will be through someone who is Lebanese."[14] The appropriation of the outside—now global—is, indeed, worthy of Sedgwick, if far less concerned about the classroom. Of course Spivak's transcendent critical selfhood professes to be no less driven by grand movements of social history (racism, sexism, immigration), even as she permits herself such "personal" asides as the following: "In February of 1991, I was in a pretty villa on Lake Como, owned by the Rockefellers, where I hope to be again. We were conferring on intercultural performance."[15]

My subsequent parody of a resignation is, in contrast, an example of an intercultural performance that does not come off. I was in no position to dazzle. I had only the inside. The Fulbright award had given me at least social access to some outside, but it never ceased to be dubious, access choked by the conditions of teaching in Saudi Arabia. Finally, the award itself, even if articulated within a transnational framework, was only intelligible as an award in American terms. I had no other educational structure in which to try to make good some understanding of myself as a professional subject—albeit for the moment, as a provincial within the institutional hierarchy of higher education, I was somehow distinctive or distinguished as a political subject. It felt no more possible for me to resign from *anywhere* than it is for a postcolonial to resign from the sociopolitical formations of imperialism (or—to recall my second chapter—a dissertating subject from the latest revisionary scheme called for by her director).

The application of the postcolonial model to a far narrower academic system might seem glib. It is not. Years later in Brazil, for example, I heard of a man from Trinidad who refused to take out Brazilian citizenship when it was decreed by the government that faculty at all universities must be citizens in order to continue to receive medical benefits. How long could he afford to hold out? The man who told me this did not know. He himself was from Malta, and had been working in Brazil for thirty years without having to relinquish his citizenship. But the previous year family circumstances forced him to sign up and become a Brazilian. I never knew him well enough to be able to say whether he felt he had written himself out of one narrative more than he felt he had written himself into another.

Academics do this sort of thing all the time, and more have to use their national signatures in most untheoretical ways, I think, than a purely American understanding of academic structure typically comprehends. Even as this structure is itself increasingly mandated to face its global interconnection, right down at the level where students are taught, there is little attention paid to how such interconnection already shapes both the lives of the people doing the teaching and the standards of their disci-plines.[16] In a searching review of three books on American higher educa-tion in the *Times Literary Supplement*, John Sutherland has a sharp comment on a footnote to Homi Bhabha's chapter on "Postcolonial Criti-cism" in one of the books. Sutherland's comment is worth quoting at length. After citing Bhabha's acknowledgment of a question once put to him in a Cambridge, Massachusetts, bar by Stephen Greenblatt, Suther-land continues:

> The Sussex and Berkeley professors are 2,000 miles equidistant from their home departments. It does not matter who picks up the tab—the *per diem* will cover that, just as the institution will pay all other conference expenses. And so—in the interval between panels—as they sip their drinks, the new his-toricist and the postcolonialist ponder the mysterious geometry of signifiers. And out of such musings emerges *Redrawing the Boundaries* (paid for by the MLA out of conference fees). The book is addressed to the profession at large as a low-priced how-to manual for the teachers. The wisdom idly given birth in the Cambridge bar will ultimately fall on the classroom as doctrine.[17]

Much depends, I suppose, on how far you get to be from home. Just as much may depend on how far you are able to be from the classroom. If you get far enough from home, you do not have to worry about the class-room. In the global view, everything fits—from the stray anecdote to the cutting edge of the disciplinary boundary. It is only locally that things break down once more, and division seems to be built into the very nature of professional life. Each nation now contracts to the size of a college cam-pus (or a department), sufficient unto itself. There are limits to strain against again. In order for there to be big interdisciplinary pictures, even the most fervent postcolonialist must admit, there have to be hundreds of thousands of little homes for them, and regular classroom hours all se-mester in the same old rooms.

Back home, that is, you must accustom yourself once more to one life where, especially if the campus is far off the international circuit, the rep-resentation is simpler, the issues more private, and the transcripts more hidden. It will not be necessary to do more than teach. The critical per-formance you can be expected to give will be appropriately modest. The writing you can try to produce must be, so to speak, doctrinally sound. Available fictions about the most commonplace circumstances of your professional life will have nothing to say about such things as letters of resignation. Happy or not, everybody is resigned. But nobody resigns.

❧

One of the most unusual things about Mary McCarthy's once-famous academic novel, *The Groves of Academe,* is that a resignation letter is at the center of it. The novel, in fact, is framed by letters. The hero, Henry Mulcahy, receives a letter from the president of Jocelyn College at the beginning of the book informing him of his dismissal. The president, Maynard Hoar, shocks everyone at the end when he discloses that he has sent a letter of resignation to the board of trustees. The text of neither of these letters is given in the narrative, which in a sense traces how one man's letter in which he loses his job is transformed into another man's letter in which he resigns from his job.

The most powerful resignation letter is written by Alma Fortune, a colleague of Mulcahy's, who never expected her or anyone to go so far in the support for him that he is carefully trying to orchestrate. Mulcahy pleads with Alma to reconsider. Once she goes, he maintains, so will Hoar's conscience. Her role is as his "gadfly." Alma is being too selfish. "I learned long ago," Alma replies, "that one can't bargain in these affairs. If one wants to be effective, one hands in one's resignation and clears out. There's no other way for a man or an institution to learn that one is serious than to learn it too late."[18]

By today's conventions, Alma is hard to fix. A widow, she is not exactly a feminist and not exactly not. "She was both extremely outspoken and extremely reserved; her personality was posted with all sorts of No trespassing signs and crisscrossed with electric fences, which repelled the intruder with a smart shock" (111). It is not clear what professorial rank she has. The narrative exhibits no interest in how Alma will survive after she resigns, although Mulcahy accuses her of thinking she will have no trouble in getting another job. Other than a strong conviction about serious actions (including some assessment of what they cost), Alma appears to have no discernable motive for her letter.

Her belief in the consequences of her action (although she admits that she does not expect her departure alone to save Mulcahy) makes especially strange reading at present. Budget cuts abound in higher education. State legislators denounce tenure. Today, the administration might be delighted to accept Alma's letter so they could either hire someone younger and cheaper or just transpose her "line" into an adjunct job. The difference between firing and resignation is less decidable now, as reliance on part-time or temporary staff increases and a computation of costs overcomes a vocabulary of ideals. Most striking (even if President Hoar pleads financial considerations to justify Mulcahy's firing) is that Alma expects through her action to engage this vocabulary directly—as she does, immediately, when Mulcahy himself feels rebuked because he has chosen not to resign.

Does Alma have a Ph.D.? Does she have tenure? Is she a full professor? McCarthy's narrative is blissfully indifferent to such questions. Of course one reason is that Jocelyn College is equally indifferent. As a colleague explains to Alma, the problem from Jocelyn's point of view is that Mulcahy is a scholar (with a Ph.D.), not that he is not: great learning "opens up too great a hiatus, as in Hen's case, between the student and the instructor. . . . we regard advanced degrees as a liability, if anything" (127). In the 1990s there may still be colleges such as Jocelyn. (McCarthy had taught at Bard and Sarah Lawrence before she wrote the novel.) But it is difficult to believe that even the most progressive Eastern liberal arts campuses have not been profoundly affected today by the vast and intricate professionalization of every discipline.

The imperative to have a Ph.D. is, all by itself, one way that any field or any institution can erect its own criteria for credentials or for certification. Forty years after the publication of *The Groves of Academe* there are far more ways available to keep people away from the tenured interior of academic life, just as there appear to be more ways to let them go out occasionally (on conferences, sabbaticals, or leaves), once inside. Another striking thing about the novel, however, occurs during the spring "moment" when everybody seems to be "boarding the gravy train" (219). One man gets a Fulbright to Lebanon. Another marries a rich widow. Still another receives a Rockefeller. The relation between the inside and outside of academic life here finally becomes puzzling. If in some ways the relation is precious and constricted compared to today, in other ways it is open and expansive.

The difference can be characterized very simply: a person can resign. The resignation letter, I think, marks the intersection of private and public energies in academic life. Writing out of the intolerable circumstances of the one usually involves passing into some hopeful alignment with the other, even if it is just another teaching job somewhere else. One way to assess how academic life has changed in the past forty years would be to pose the following question: is the possibility of writing a letter of resignation still part of the script of academic life? (Adjuncts of course are not in position to write such a letter, which alone illuminates their dubious relation to the script.) Nothing is more remarkable about *The Groves of Academe* than that everyone acts as if such letters, no matter how unusual, could be written as part of the discursive conditions in which ordinary work takes place. At some point, for some people, a letter of resignation *makes sense*. Alma is one of those people.

Yet how to clarify the precise sense such a letter makes? McCarthy's narrative cannot accomplish it, except in personal terms and then only by contrast to Alma's younger colleague, Domna, a Russian who teaches Russian literature, while fretting and agonizing throughout over the morality of her actions. At one point Domna decides that she should always ask herself, what would Tolstoy think. Alma laughs. "It's not at all the same with Dostoevsky. I don't give a damn what he thinks." In Dostoevsky, she continues, "it's all *there* in the novels; there's no injunction to action, no trailing moral imperatives, no direct preaching . . . the morality's inseparable from the form" (252).

Just so, Alma resigns. Her letter is merely her action expressed as writing. She could just as well not have written it at all. People who resign, I think, do not bother much about writing. Too much bother would mean too much form, and too much form would pull away from the morality of the action. So, for another example, Donald Hall simply mentions that almost twenty years ago he quit teaching. He doesn't dwell on why, although his detestation at the "chore" of reading composition papers shows through.[19] If we wanted to insist that he give some account anyway, I think he would respond with the moral force of his whole life. In Hall's case much of this force impels him to return home to his roots in rural New Hampshire.

To those of us, on the other hand, for whom morality is irrevocably separated from form, or, worse, for whom form has fatally assumed the role of a seductive action in whose clutches we conspire, there remains instead only the performance of various kinds of disguise. Why, for example, after posing the question of whether or not his life "beyond the tenure track" has been worth it, does James Phelan conclude his book by citing Joyce's Molly Bloom?[20] Has academic life prevented him from uttering his own "yes" in his own name? Or should we suspect that somewhere in this "yes" is a "no?" More certainly, there is a text.

For academics, there is always an available text. Perhaps in academic fictions letters of resignation are suppressed because they signal the end of textuality as well as of employment. Academics often resemble the condition of the soldier (in an old joke from World War II) who haunts the parade grounds, picking up pieces of paper, looking at them, and declaring, "This ain't it." Finally, a sergeant takes him to a psychiatrist, who pronounces him unfit for service and hands the soldier a pink slip to discharge him. "That's it!" the man cries. Academics, in contrast, would prefer to write the slip themselves. Life must go on, no less so if sometimes it appears more urgent to write it all out than to live it.

Charles Altieri criticizes Paul Smith's study of the subject because "He fails to make the necessary step from resistance as the way active agency manifests itself in political terms to resistance as the condition of being an active agent."[21] It seems to me that academic life enjoins exactly this step: a condition of being an academic is resistance to being one. Resistance takes many forms, compliance foremost among them, particularly compliance to the ways in which dominant discourse writes subordination. Another form is one I have tried to demonstrate throughout this book: the sort of luxuriant transcendence so openly performed by institutionalized elites according to the latest critical scripts, including nowadays the queer and the postcolonial.

What I performed over a decade ago in my letters of resignation was a species of resistance the more elusive because, I think, it enacted the inner logic of a sovereign practice without any of its outward occasion. My guess is that many academics write out of this sort of logic all the time. They write letters, parodies, and hidden transcripts. Nobody but friends sees them. Of course these people need the security of a job. But they also abide in distinctively insecure circumstances where it is often idle to distinguish between being resigned and resigning, or even between being in subordination and being insubordinate. Which was Sedgwick when she performed queer at Duke? Which was I when I wrote mockingly in Saudi Arabia? Who can tell? Sometimes you have to be from the outside to tell the difference. Or, even if, with luck, you get to the outside, you still might discover that you cannot go undisguised.

There is a lovely moment near the end of *The Groves of Academe* corresponding to similar ones in many academic novels that so commonly wind up repudiating the whole setting. Keogh, a gruff old leftist poet, has appeared at Jocelyn's big poetry conference; we may be sure that he never wrote a dissertation. Alas, he gets drawn into more of the politics surrounding Mulcahy than he can stand. So when he spots Domna, and thinks of speaking to her, he inwardly cries out: *Keogh, keep out of this or they will get you.* Maybe, he thinks, all are "very nice, high-minded-scrupulous people," although "always emending, penciling, erasing" (295). But no. Although he is scheduled to be somewhere at this hour, he signals to a tall blonde on a bicycle and throws two pamphlets the president had given him in a trash can.

Keogh's "agency" is not of an academic sort. An academic might or might not be engaged by the local politics. There are, after all, many ways to express engagement, including purporting to stand aloof. Furthermore, an academic might or might not signal to the blonde. These days, though, a male academic would probably be wise to keep walking. However, most academics, I believe, whether inclined to keep to the conference schedule or not, would be hard put to throw away the pamphlets.

The president had given the pamphlets to Keogh after summoning him into his office in order to inquire about Mulcahy's communist past. The pamphlets are in fact two articles—one specific, the other more theoretical—that the president has published in order to establish himself as a "liberal pundit." Yet Keogh discards them, and with them, not only a whole form of political discourse, but the academic context for it. He's not an academic. He doesn't care what might be discovered in virtually any text. Distinguished or lowly, it is as if each one testifies to a remorseless, compromising activity which is all of a piece.

Much as I admire Keogh's example, however, I can't repeat it. Indeed, I believe it is almost impossible for an academic to avoid making an argument for the value of just about anything written. Even the most disingenuous things matter, especially if they are those of the president, although it's hard to evaluate them in a positive way. Hardest of all, perhaps, is to describe what follows from the realization that what is written—memo or pamphlet, it ultimately makes no difference—is about *you.* One thing that follows, though, is the wish that you had written it yourself, even as you must acknowledge that if you wanted to remain on campus you could have written only in disguise.

Notes

Introduction

1. Catherine Stimpson, "Dirty Minds, Dirty Bodies, Clean Speech," *Michigan Quarterly Review* 32 (Summer 1993): 320.

2. Stanley Fish, "The Unbearable Ugliness of Volvos," in *English Inside and Out: The Places of Literary Criticism,* ed. Susan Gubar and Jonathan Kamholtz (New York: Routledge, 1993), 108. Fish makes the same charge of mean actions couched in noble principle that Stimpson does. "In the academy, the lower the act, the higher the principle invoked to justify it" (106). A less emphatic, focused rehearsal of this same moment can be found at the end of James Phelan's academic memoir, *Beyond the Tenure Track* (Columbus: Ohio State University Press, 1991), when, after noting that to care so much about professional "validation" through publication seems "a sign of the infection," he writes that "I find myself shaking my head at my socialization, at the power the need for the external validation seems to have (had?) over me" (216–17).

Adam Begley does not mention Fish (or Phelan) in a piece in *Lingua Franca* on Duke University professors who have sharpened the cutting edge by writing autobiography, but I think both Stimpson and Fish must be understood in the context of a professional critique whose repudiation of academic life is so profound that it can only lead out of that life entirely. Begley finds Jane Tompkins working as a cook on a two-year leave. He does not claim that Cathy Davidson (who explains the turn to autobiography as the result of an aging professorate) must travel to Japan. But he does quote Frank Lentricchia, although the depths of Lentricchia's estrangement from all his academic circumstances in *The Edge of Night* (New York: Random House, 1994) are difficult to illustrate by quotation. "The exceptional life is surely worth recording," Begley concludes, "and we all cherish extraordinary accounts of ordinary lives. But what about the mass of middling lives, ably but not brilliantly exhibited?" See Begley, "The I's Have It: Duke's Moi Critics Expose Themselves," *Lingua Franca* 4 (March/April 1994): 59. The answer everywhere suggested by his I's can be given more simply than Begley is willing to allow: middling academic lives are filled with more petty dispute, self-indulgence, and fantasized transcendence than Duke would dream.

A far more strenuously theoretical response to the question is given in Daniel O'Hara, *Radical Parody: American Culture and Critical Agency after Foucault* (New York: Columbia University Press, 1992). O'Hara's final chapter is devoted to Lentricchia's critical practice, or rather his critical identity as a guide to, if not a transcendence of, practice. As O'Hara comments, with typical lavishness: "Amid all the purely professional processes for grinding the particular achievements of writers into grist for the latest mills of careerism, celebrity, and professionalism to no end, I find this truly artistic performance of imaginative generosity that still sees all the historical and political limitations, to be courageous and bracing, an aesthetic use of the collective archive of creative exempla for constructively socializing and humanizing purposes—that is, the anchoring of our culture of critical identity in the plural authority of 'oneself'" (268).

3. James Slevin, "The Politics of the Profession," in *An Introduction to Composition Studies*, ed. Erika Lindeman and Gary Tate (New York: Oxford University Press, 1991), 157. In an earlier footnote, to a description of the writing program included by the English chair in his letter offering a position to the candidate, Slevin states: "It goes without saying that I can barely unpack all that is going on here. I leave much to my readers" (157). Yet how much can be safely left to one's readers, especially in matters of this kind? On behalf of my own readers, in the following pages I leave much less. Most I have tried to consign to footnotes, along with my own hope that I not be judged to have left more.

4. Charles Altieri, "What Is at Stake in Confessional Criticism," in *Confessions of the Critics*, ed. H. Aram Veeser (New York: Routledge, 1996), 58. See the four ways Altieri commends autobiographical criticism at its best, especially the third, or ethical, mode, about which he writes as follows: "autobiography paradoxically provides a counter to fantasies of powerful, autonomous selves, because it forces us to confront how determined we are by contingent forces that we cannot control" (57).

5. Of course nothing personal rebukes a discourse like sex. Consider the following exchange between Leon Botstein, Joan Blythe, and William Kerrigan, from a recent popular discussion about sexual harassment:

> BOTSTEIN: Let me say this: I think sexual relations trigger a set of ethical obligations.
> BLYTHE: Ethical obligations?
> BOTSTEIN: Ethical obligations.
> KERRIGAN: Ethical obligations?

See "Forum: New Rules about Sex on Campus," *Harper's*, September 1993, 38. Botstein goes on to try to argue that in having an affair with a student, a teacher is being unfair to the others, and would be as "slanted" as a judge in a violin contest if his grandmother entered. Blythe disagrees; judgment is always personal. Kerrigan argues that someone who has sex with another might well be in the best position to make a judgment or write a letter of recommendation.

This dialogue is an excellent example not only of how the issue of sexual harassment is normally taken to be, just by virtue of being an issue, a criticism of American higher education; Blythe and Kerrigan, here, advance the critique by effectively arguing that Botstein (a college president) has standards too smug and "academic" (a word they don't use). The exchange also discloses how a consummately personal question is inexorably transformed into a textual one—a letter of recommendation—by a group of academics.

The process appears at once more intricately and more self-consciously in Jane Gallop's new book on being charged with sexual harassment—right to the very end, when Gallop remarks that the "spectacle" suggested by her "tabloid title" is precisely the spectacle she desires to make of herself, albeit producing sensations that represent "the best kind." See Jane Gallop, *Feminist Accused of Sexual Harassment* (Durham: Duke University Press, 1997), 101. Unfortunately her fascinating performance appeared too late for me to discuss it in any detail either here or in the following chapters.

6. Richard Ohmann, *English in America* (New York: Oxford University Press, 1976), 254.

7. James C. Scott, *Domination and the Arts of Resistance: Hidden Transcripts* (New Haven: Yale University Press, 1990), 17.

8. One reason they do is because many administrators were once professors—and many professors will one day be administrators. Therefore, the one is "dominant," and the other "subordinate," in a sense much less fixed than that Scott considers. Nonetheless, see especially his "paper thin theory of hegemony" on how groups legitimate the conditions that subordinate them, especially 82–83.

9. Scott, *Domination*, 114–15. An especially torturous example of trying to rewrite one's own exclusion is provided by the chapter "The Academic Thing" in Sande Cohen, *Academia and the Luster of Capital* (Minneapolis: University of Minnesota Press, 1993). Cohen details two job searches in which he was personally involved. But names must be suppressed, the institutions deleted, and, in the space where one would expect him to write autobiographically, Cohen instead attempts to overpower mundanities with a formidable theoretical grasp. Hence, asked during an interview whether he believes in affirmative action, Cohen responds thus: "Sent into space aboard this piece of libidinal academic surplus hate, I was swept up in what Gremias has called 'practical diffusion in a mythical manifestation,' the meaning of which is partially found in considering acts of intellectual targeting: an event where everything is overdetermined, the revisions operative in rationalizing the 'right to exclude' and control" (45). I conclude that some individuals experience their own exclusion so totally that it simply cannot be rewritten except as the very totality that authorizes the exclusion.

10. Scott, *Domination*, 58. For an example of how corporate business demonstrates its sensitivity to the inevitable resistance it elicits, see Daniel Harris, "The Aesthetic of the Computer," *Salmagundi* 101–2 (Winter–Spring 1994): 173–81. Studying the wild creativity of screen-saver programs and software programs generally, Harris demonstrates as follows: "By inspiring a sense of community united by irreverence, by a shared bond of insolence and sarcasm, the aesthetic of the computer allows the worker to participate in a form of make-believe disobedience" (179).

For a general perspective on the politics of discipline in the workspace, see the chapter "Bodies of Knowledge" in John Fiske's *Power Plays, Power Works* (New York: Verso, 1993). Fiske remarks, for example, as follows: "The art of making do extends into the art of making 'our' space within 'their' space" (70). The problem indicated by Harris's screen-savers, however, is that "they" are so good at anticipating "our" improvisations that our creativity can become a resource of their discipline.

11. Reed Way Dasenbrock, "What Is English Anyway?" *College English* 55 (September 1993): 546. One of the books under review is by Evan Watkins, *Work Time: English Departments and the Circulation of Cultural Value* (Stanford: Stanford University Press, 1989). Of it, Dasenbrock writes: "What baffles me here is not the failure—since I don't see any way to succeed—but the ambition. It puzzles me to see someone like Watkins dwell so comfortably within the conventions of academic discourse yet so clearly feel that he should be doing something else" (543). I make the same point in the introduction to *Conspiring with Forms: Life in Academic Texts* (Athens: University of Georgia, 1992). For another kind of example of a comfort similar to, if more provocative than, that enjoyed by Watkins, see Margaret Talbot's account of the sexual harassment charges brought against Jane Gallop for her teaching methods, "A Most Dangerous Method," *Lingua Franca* 4 (January/February 1994): 1, 24–40.

12. For a brilliant, elaborate parody of the amplitude of this position, see Eva Bueno, "O'Camping at Harvard," *North Dakota Quarterly* 34 (Fall 1996): 113–23. For an authoritative discussion of its origins in celebrity as well as academic culture, see David Shumway, "The Star System in Literary Studies," *PMLA* 112 (January 1997): 85–100. The celebrity character of present academic life is mentioned several times in Veeser's collection of essays, *Confessions of the Critics*, but nowhere are its consequences taken up at any length.

13. Daniel O'Hara and Donald Pease, "An Interview with Frank Lentricchia," *Boundary* 2 21.2 (1994): 28. To Lentricchia and his interviewers, it is as if the autobiographical text were in the position of a hidden transcript, as against the dominant position of the scholarly text on modernism. What happens, in effect, is that during the course of the interview the autobiographical volume is discursively transferred, if not transformed, into dominance. Although no one quite states it this way, Lentricchia, it turns out, since he is a major figure in the profession, cannot produce a hidden transcript! No one discusses how his prac-

tice might devolve upon the great majority who, for the same reasons, can produce only hidden transcripts. Charles Altieri's critique of Lentricchia's autobiographical sketch touches on this last point; see Veeser, *Confessions*, 55–67.

14. Robert Hughes, *Culture of Complaint* (New York: Oxford University Press, 1993), 68.

15. Charles Altieri, *Canons and Consequences: Reflections on the Ethical Force of Imaginative Ideals* (Evanston: Northwestern University Press, 1990), 207. Altieri is commenting on the centrality of resistance in Paul Smith's *Discerning the Subject* (Minneapolis: University of Minnesota Press, 1990). He goes on to clarify the politics of such activity thus: "Agents act politically not by projecting goals for the collective but by pursuing their own needs to lessen the pressure of contradiction and, if we add a touch of Lyotard, by seeking full expression for that which might allow them a less contradictory, less victimized social identity." This is not to explain, Altieri hastens to add, why one must only be an active agent by resisting, quite apart from politics, as Smith appears to assume.

16. Patricia Williams, *The Alchemy of Race and Rights* (Cambridge: Harvard University Press, 1991), 50. She concludes thus: "The problem, of course, will be that in the hierarchy of law-review citation, the article in the newspaper will have more authoritative weight about me, as a so-called 'primary resource,' than I will have; it will take precedence over my own citation of the unverifiable testimony of my own speech." I know of few more acute examples than this account of how the hidden transcript—whether, here, against the society or against the discipline—must stay hidden in order for the dominant script to function. Moreover, it is made clear everywhere in the book that this script is written by bidding individual subjectivity either to rewrite or unwrite itself.

17. Jane Gallop, *Around 1981: Academic Feminist Literary Theory* (New York: Routledge, 1992), 10.

18. Gerald Graff, "Preaching to the Converted," in Gubar and Kamholtz, *English Inside and Out*, 114. He continues: "For a generation now, the humanities have actually penalized narrow specialization and reserved their highest rewards for work that propounds sweeping cultural theories and broad interdisciplinary generalizations, work that promises to revise the paradigm for thinking about its subject." Given such a circumstance, one can only wonder about the nature of "work" that lacks so much as the opportunity or logic for specialization. No wonder James Phelan, for example, on a recruiting trip for prospective Ohio State graduate students, makes the following comment when he visits Corpus Christi State and speaks to one of the English department's three members, trained as a Renaissance scholar, who is in fact responsible with her four-course-a-semester load for all of British literature: "Our conversation made me feel that my job is a sinecure." See Phelan, *Beyond the Tenure Track*, 69.

19. The outcry over political correctness can be understood not only as a struggle waged between the public and academics over the question of how

ideologically uniform American higher education either is or ought to be, but also within the hierarchy of academic institutions. For a convenient collection of articles, see Paul Berman, ed., *Debating P.C.: The Controversy over Political Correctness on College Campuses* (New York: Laurel, 1992) and, even better, Jeffrey Williams, ed., *PC Wars: Politics and Theory in the Academy* (New York: Routledge, 1994).

Institutional asymmetry with respect to this question is rarely expressed. I am thinking, for example, of William Kerrigan's comment: "The decentered multi-cultural curriculum is just the particular way in which the upper tier of [the whole educational system] is now collapsing." See Mark Edmundson, ed., *Wild Orchids and Trotsky: Messages from American Universities* (New York: Penguin, 1993), 167. The lower tier, even as it labors to establish the same kind of curriculum, looks up at signs of collapse with some amusement, I think, or tries to, just as large segments of the broader public do.

20. Scott, *Domination*, 200. He continues: "If formal political organization is the realm of elites (for example, lawyers, politicians, revolutionaries, political bosses), of written records (for example, resolutions, declarations, news stories, petitions, lawsuits), and of public action, infrapolitics is, by contrast, the realm of informal leadership and nonelites, of conversation and oral discourse, and of surreptitious resistance." Scott also notes that what counts as infrapolitical depends upon the society—hence, under tyranny, it is political life itself.

See also John Fiske: "The ability to masquerade or to dissemble identity is a survival tactic; it is a defensive power by which workers maintain their identities against those required by management, by which women hold theirs against patriarchy, or gays and lesbians theirs against heterosexism; it is the power of children to keep secret areas of identity beyond the knowledge of teachers and parents." See Fiske, *Power*, 68.

21. Edmundson, *Wild Orchids*, 91.

22. Cohen, *Academia*, 16. He continues as follows: "The incorporeality of much linguistic presentation, where semantic effects are virtually registered without analytic discussion, may well acquire its academic 'force' by the rigid nonrecognition of meanings that come from elsewhere." The personal, one could say, always comes from elsewhere.

23. Cohen, *Academia*, 51. Compare David Bromwich: "Against the bureaucrats of sexual, racial, ethnic, and religious purity, who invoke with such misleading intent the language of community, a resistance that amounts to hatred may be the sanest feeling to cherish. It gives, at least, some edge to whatever integral humanity one must call upon, and serves as a reminder that the caring groups are really hard as nails: they want to destroy us, each of us, and always for the sake of all." See Bromwich, *Politics by Other Means: Higher Education and Group Thinking* (New Haven: Yale University Press, 1992), 23. The difference is that whereas Cohen reads the academic structure itself, Bromwich reads only the current corruption of it by politics (more accurately, the failed politics of the

whole country). Consequently, Bromwich is not inclined to examine very searchingly how the academy could have accommodated itself so readily to being politicized, and therefore he lacks any specific vision about how "resistance" could function, or at least possess some "edge."

24. Michel de Certeau, *The Practice of Everyday Life* (Berkeley: University of California Press, 1984), 30. This point immediately precedes his better-known distinction between strategies and tactics. A hidden transcript is by definition a tactic, which lacks the options "of planning general strategy and viewing the adversary as a whole within a district [sic], visible, and objectifiable space. It operates in isolated actions, blow by blow. . . . What it wins it cannot keep" (37). At the present time, for example, my department has evolved a ten-point form for each semester's evaluation of non-tenured faculty, with options ranging from "very strongly agree" to "not applicable." The final point is the following: "The instructor established an effective learning community."

25. Candace Lang, "Autocritique," in Veeser, *Confessions*, 45.

26. Charles Altieri, "What Is at Stake in Confessional Criticism," in Veeser, *Confessions*, 66. Compare David Damrosch, *We Scholars: Changing the Culture of the University* (Cambridge: Harvard University Press, 1995). In the figure of the solitary researcher, Damrosch in effect concedes something suspiciously akin to alienation to be the defining condition of academic life; see especially chapter 3, "The Scholar as Exile." Damrosch tries to rewrite alienation as community. Rather paradoxically, I see, in contrast, the essence of community to be that it can only be rewritten as alienation.

27. It is hard to know which is the case represented by Eve Kosofsky Sedgwick's statement: "The people I teach gay and lesbian studies to are also the people whom, when I can do it, I do gay and lesbian activism with." See Sedgwick, "Notes toward Queer Performativity," in Gubar and Kamholtz, *English Inside and Out*, 127. Are we to believe, then, that none of the students in Sedgwick's classes offers any resistance to her subject? In the next sentence she mentions graduate students. Perhaps we are to believe that Sedgwick's entire teaching load consists of teaching gay and lesbian studies to graduate students (and now, as she implies, teaching them how to write essays like she does).

28. Cohen, *Academia*, 35. He means that yet more committees will be formed instead. Although Cohen never cites Stanley Fish, such a contention makes contact with his de-politicized or "pragmatic" position; Fish states, for example, in his chapter on anti-professionalism, "there are no goals and reasons that are not institutional, that do not follow from the already in-place assumptions, stipulated definitions, and categories of understanding of a socially organized activity." See Fish, *Doing What Comes Naturally: Change, Rhetoric, and the Practice of Theory in Literary and Legal Studies* (Durham: Duke University Press, 1990), 242–43. On the contrary, one could reply to Fish: hidden transcripts, no matter how they can (or must) be understood in institutional terms, do not "follow" at all insofar as they have some political object or other public-spirited aim of "problematiz-

ing." Often they merely express a sheer conviction of personal singularity—as presumably Fish himself means to, in his English Institute paper, "The Unbearable Ugliness of Volvos" (cited above), reprinted as the last chapter in Fish, *There's No Such Thing as Free Speech: And It's a Good Thing, Too* (New York: Oxford University Press, 1994).

29. This is not the case with e-mail posts, or at least (depending upon the system, list, or program) not in the same way as the written word. Electronic mail seems at first glance to have the potential for altering the whole nature of written communication—and, with it, discursive authority. Why write letters when you can use e-mail? Why not think of a writing so immediate it is more akin to speaking? Why even bother about authority? Hence, we have quickly grown accustomed to such cybercalls to communicative renewal as the following: "[T]he new formations of academic thought that emerge at the interface between scholarly reportage and the performative gesture hold significant and promising power for rethinking what a university is and ought to be, here at the close of the mechanical age. . . . We no longer live in a world in which information conserves itself primarily in textual objects called books." See Allucquere Rosanne Stone, *The War of Desire and Technology at the Close of the Mechanical Age* (Boston: MIT Press, 1995), 177.

Yet we do, I believe, continue to live in a world where the material text remains the crucial source of meaning and significance. Although Michael Crichton's popular novel of sexual harassment, *Disclosure* (New York: Knopf, 1993) begins with an e-mail message, it is printed as a memo. Moreover, despite the climactic virtual reality database adventure, the perfidy of the villain could never have been proven had certain memos she sent by e-mail not been materially available and transmittable by fax. Electronic communication, in other words, can be recoverable in the form of a written transcript, and origin, if not authorship, can be located. There is no doubt, however, that, as Sherry Turkle states, "[l]ife on the screen makes it very easy to present oneself as other than one is in real life." See Turkle, *Identity in the Age of the Internet* (New York: Simon & Schuster, 1995), 228. It is one thing to write in disguise because you are not subordinate to anyone, and quite another thing to write in disguise because you are. What networks of control and circuits of power this difference will play itself out in will determine the political future of electronic communication.

30. Edward Said, "Identity, Authority, and Freedom," in *The Future of Academic Freedom*, ed. Louis Menand (Chicago: University of Chicago Press, 1996), 227. Said goes on to invoke the model of "inhabiting the academic and cultural space provided by school and university" on the image of—of all things—a traveler. A finer prospect could not be imagined. Alas, however, Said never pauses to wonder how many are actually free to be so mobile, nor to question whether such a model in fact makes for a coherent academic narrative, whose terms may have to be rooted and bounded in order to be academic in the first place.

Chapter One

1. Edward Allen, *Mustang Sally* (New York: W. W. Norton, 1992), 125.

2. Especially notable in sexual harassment cases is how often the unquestioned authority of the written word is at their center. Thus, one of the two students bringing charges against Jane Gallop focuses on two letters of recommendation that Gallop refused to write. See Margaret Talbot, "A Most Dangerous Method," *Lingua Franca* 4 (January/February 1994): 36–37. Or, Richard Bernstein finds the University of New Hampshire campus full of bulletin boards and posters on the dangers of rape, as the director of the Affirmative Action Office strives for a stronger policy statement on harassment, following the suspension of a professor for certain remarks made to several women in his classes. See Bernstein, "Guilty if Charged," *New York Review of Books*, January 13, 1994, 14, substantially reprinted in *Dictatorship of Virtue: Multiculturalism, Diversity, and the American Future* (New York: Knopf, 1994).

Although her book is an argument against the fear and intolerance of sexual harassment charges and pieties, Katie Roiphe expresses the same assumptions. Take Back the Night speak-outs, for example, "follow conventions as strict as any sonnet sequence or villanelle." See Roiphe, *The Morning After: Sex, Fear, and Feminism on Campus* (Boston: Little, Brown and Company, 1993), 36. Similarly, her reading of date-rape pamphlets as beginning to sound "like Victorian guides to conduct" (66) attempts to intervene in the authority of something written by comparing it to a disused form, or else, as when she compares a theoretically trendy classmate to a woman of high fashion buying the latest hat in *Vogue* (129), by dissolving the written word back into life.

The result of these disputes is that critics of the excesses of sexual harassment usually find themselves overreading, because they are comfortable with things in writing, while proponents are underwriting, because they would prefer to have things spoken. Bernstein cites an excellent example in a campus-wide letter from the coordinator of the UNH women's studies program (in which she writes that the First Amendment is "just another yoke around our necks"). The coordinator responds in a letter to the editor that the letter had nothing to do with Bernstein's particular case and was quoted out of context; Bernstein should have telephoned her. Bernstein denies the contentions and tries to expand the context. See "'Guilty if Charged': An Exchange," *New York Review of Books*, March 24, 1994, 59–60. The implicit problem in all of this might be phrased in the following way: is there a proper form for private experience?

3. See Roiphe on the rhetorical violence in the language of Catherine MacKinnon, perhaps the leading spokeswoman for the horrors of violence against women, *Morning After*, 150–51. On the widely shared vocabularies of sex and violence, see an especially trenchant commentary by Louis Menand, "The War of All against All, *New Yorker*, March 14, 1994, 74–85.

Under the circumstances, the following story about William Empson is not without a certain charm, because he appears to be oblivious to any but an older vocabulary that disdains both violence and sex. A twenty-two-year-old at Cambridge, Empson never received his degree after his maid discovered a contraceptive in his room. Empson explained to the disciplinary board that he was sleeping with a lady don, and suggested that they would surely prefer that he did not get her pregnant.

4. Billy Wright Dziech and Linda Weiner, *The Lecherous Professor. Sexual Harassment on Campus*, 2d ed. (Urbana: University of Illinois Press, 1990), xxiii–xxiv.

5. James C. Scott, *Domination and the Arts of Resistance: Hidden Transcripts* (New Haven: Yale University Press, 1990), 102–3. My purpose in citing Scott here is to explicate a structural situation rather than a social or political one. The ideological factors (defined by, but not limited to, feminism) that make *The Lecherous Professor* a writing of the dominant are another matter. Scott's point is merely that in power relations there is an official story, and, moreover, that some such stories can purchase their power by including remarkably varied elements. I take Dziech's citation of the letter to be an example of this.

6. Not to say the fact (if not the power) of autobiographical writing, for exactly the same reason. Charles Altieri suggests that this "turn" can be explained because "critics want to displace into the realm of the personal the disturbing fact that they are among the most intelligent members of a democratic society that grants them privileges but does not have any set of values which might justify those privileges (in contrast with its values about medicine, say)." See Altieri, "What Is at Stake in Confessional Criticism," in *Confessions of the Critics*, ed. H. Aram Veeser (New York: Routledge, 1996), 66.

In this respect, Jane Gallop's recent attempt to recuperate for a re-eroticized notion of pedagogy the spectacle of herself kissing a student in public expresses, I think, a kind of aggression against this same society. See Gallop, *Feminist Accused of Sexual Harassment* (Durham: Duke University Press, 1997).

7. Dziech and Weiner, *Lecherous Professor*, 48. This statement is from a section on Diffused Institutional Authority, in which elsewhere the language is even more suggestive. For example, the following passage, in italics: "The critical point is this: because the social structure of the university is loose, ambiguous, and poorly defined, the power structure of the university is also loose, ambiguous, shifting, and poorly defined" (47). In more explicit gendered terms, the problem with the university according to the authors is that its organization is too decentered, or "female," and therefore needs to become stronger and more phallic. But of course something very much like this same logic is expressed on micro-levels of the structure by the action of the sexual harasser himself. For a gendered reading of another book on sex in academic life—this time classroom dynamics—see Jane Gallop, "The Teacher's Breasts," *Discourse* 17 (Fall 1994): 3–15.

8. So it goes, I think, throughout the world, country by country, where so

many sexual practices and cultural values simply cannot be mapped onto American ones. A recent piece in the *New Republic*, to take still another example, sketches the trials of an American woman in Russia within a language that does not admit "women" (except as derogatory), only either *devuskhi*, girls, or *babushki*, grandmothers. See Liesl Schillinger, "Devushki!" *New Republic*, August 9, 1993, 9–10. A woman, in effect, especially at night, has to risk harassment in the company of one man or more in order not to be even more harassed by all.

See also the French friend cited by Roiphe, who maintains that the issue of control is such an American obsession—an "important point," she feels, "amid all of my friend's predictable bluster about American puritanism." See Roiphe, *Morning After*, 169–70.

9. Compare the acute reading by David Bromwich of "the language of bureaucratic prompting" regarding a faculty "loyalty oath" proposed by the administration of Clark University. "Politely to remind those who have not approved of the contents of the reminder, and who have some rights in the matter," he comments, "is indeed an attack on the freedom of action of the persons who are so addressed. In an academic setting, it is an attack on academic freedom." See Bromwich, *Politics by Other Means: Higher Education and Group Thinking* (New Haven: Yale University Press, 1992), 28.

For a still more harsh and embracing (and at times more opaque) perspective on similar degrees of academic unfreedom, see Sande Cohen, *Academia and the Luster of Capital* (Minneapolis: University of Minnesota Press, 1993), especially chapter 2. A more recent volume, edited by Louis Menand, *The Future of Academic Freedom* (Chicago: University of Chicago Press, 1996) avoids for the most part the view from the trenches, although there is the following admirably blunt statement by Menand himself: "The threat that multiculturalism and postmodernism pose to academic freedom is not epistemological or political. It is, much more banally, administrative" (17).

10. Scott, *Domination*, 205. I'm not sure, however, that, in terms of Scott's framework, the status of these confessions and recantations is completely clarified by calling them public transcripts. What Packard produces in fact is a hidden transcript in the form of a public one, at least insofar as his sincerity is so overwritten it becomes parody. The novel doesn't reveal whether anybody reads Packard's letter this way, however.

On the importance of unanimity, see Richard Bernstein's exchange with two UNH professors, where, in order to explain how one of them, or anyone else, could have taken the suspended professor's remarks as sexual harassment, he incredulously proposes the following explanation: "A university can freely fire teachers for whatever comments they might make, provided that a committee, chosen and instructed by that same university, finds those comments offensive." See Bernstein, "'Guilty if Charged': An Exchange," 60. The move to committee, in other words, even in such an apparently trivial case, is comprehended in an academic context as the move to unanimity.

11. Compare an earlier episode in the novel where, in the second semester of her freshman year, Marya takes a course in comparative religion. She despises the teacher, a balding "popinjay," popular because of his dramatic style. Marya refuses to laugh at his jokes, or to respond to his manner whereby "each time he alluded to something female he lowered his voice and added, as if off the cuff, a wry observation, meant not so much to be insulting as to be mildly teasing." See Oates, *Marya: A Life* (New York: E. P. Dutton, 1986), 156.

It develops that she receives a "humiliating" B+ for the course, and when she goes to see the instructor (who rather quickly "consents" to change her grade to an A) he remarks: "you seem like a rather grim young woman, you never smile—you look so preoccupied" (157). Marya sits in silent hatred of the man. He smiles "roguishly," he appears "satyrish." "Are you always such an ungiving young woman?" the teacher queries (158). Finally Marya speaks, lying about an illness her mother has and uttering an apology for having "offended" the man. He stammers his own apology. Before she leaves, Marya swipes a fountain pen from his cluttered desk.

The office scene is rife with a sexual tension that never breaks onto the surface. It could be read as an example of sexual harassment, and more certainly of a young woman's sexual victimization by an older, more powerful man. However, Marya is not entirely without power herself, and the protest she makes through the theft is structurally analogous to the more protracted, vulgar protest made by Sylvester later, when he is in her position and she is interpreted by Sylvester as being in the teasing professor's position.

12. See Dziech and Weiner, *The Lecherous Professor*, 138–41 especially. The way the professional crisis is transformed into the male midlife crisis is of particular interest in the argument, and typical of how in the narrative of sexual harassment the harasser is always gendered, like the institution, male, even though when faculty are comprehended in larger social and political terms they become victimized, or "impotent" (a word the text does not use in this context), and coded female. For more on "the multivalent, contested character of the categories of privacy and publicity with their gendered and racialized subtexts," see Nancy Fraser, "Sex, Lies, and the Public Sphere: Some Reflections on the Confirmation of Clarence Thomas," *Critical Inquiry* 18 (Spring 1992): 595–612.

13. Mark Edmundson, ed., *Wild Orchids and Trotsky: Messages from American Universities* (New York: Penguin Books, 1993), 3.

14. Jane Gallop, "Knot a Love Story," *Yale Journal of Criticism* 5 (Fall 1992): 214. On the erotic charge of their meetings, Gallop writes of her sense of the student, so "undefended" and "vulnerable" before her: "I feel as if he let me put his balls in my mouth." Whatever they're saying about liberal arts in America, one may be fairly sure they're not imagining this.

Or, if they are, it is only within the discourse of sexual harassment, where the gender identities would have to be reversed. Gallop's point, in contrast, is that the gender positions of student and teacher, respectively, are not coded as reversible, even if they can be, which is precisely what enables the nature of her own "hypergendered" phantasmic play explored in the essay.

In her subsequent book on being charged with sexual harassment, there is much less phantasm (in a sense the book can be read as being about the *disappointment* of the real, or inescapably social and conventionally coded) but just as much hopeful play, as in the concluding point about the "best kind" of sensation, "where knowledge and pleasure, sex and thought play off and enhance each other." See Gallop, *Feminist Accused*, 101.

Margaret Talbot makes no reference to this essay in her own about the subsequent charge of sexual harassment brought against Gallop. The real-life case rather uncannily repeats the terms of Gallop's earlier experience as Gallop herself gives them. Indeed, at least one of the graduate student accusers (who may not have had Gallop's essay available to her at the time) lives out these terms from the student position, this time embodied as female but—it could be said— hypergendered as male.

15. Edmundson, *Wild Orchids*, 263, 264. Compare John Guillory's far less adversarial point in his discussion of transference with respect to Paul de Man and his disciples: "If the institutional locus of canon formation is the school, and its instrumentality is the syllabus, the social relation between teacher and student oddly effaces its institutional conditions in producing nothing less than a kind of love: first the love of the disciple for the master, and then the love for what the master teaches, his 'teaching,' and beyond that . . . a love for the very texts the master loves." See Guillory, *Cultural Capital: The Problem of Literary Canon Formation* (Chicago: University of Chicago Press, 1993), 182. There is a problem here, though, about the effacement of institutional conditions. Some institutions efface them better than others, as well as some kinds of teaching. I think it most significant, for example, that Gallop begins her essay by mentioning that she was commuting weekly to Rice. Moreover, she and Guillory are considering graduate teaching, where, presumably, opportunities for mastery—not to say love, or sex—are greater than the sheer numbers of the undergraduate classroom permit. Sedgwick's words on this matter are both lofty and opaque—perhaps advisedly so, to the extent she is advocating less honorific, off-the-syllabus sorts of love than the type Guillory is studying.

16. John Boswell, on the contrary, remarks that the subject of homosexuality is perfectly symmetrical. The "homosexual subtext" is present in bans on student-professor sex, he maintains. "People out there are paranoid about gay men coming on to their sons." See "Forum: New Rules about Sex on Campus," *Harper's*, September 1993, 36. On this issue, see also Gallop, "The Teacher's Breasts," cited above.

17. Talbot, "Dangerous Method," 26. See also Cheryl Fish, "'Someone to Watch Over Me': Politics and Paradoxes in Academic Mentoring," in *Working-Class Women in the Academy: Laborers in the Knowledge Factory*, ed. Michelle Tokarczyk and Elizabeth Fay (Amherst: University of Massachusetts Press,

1993), 179–96. Fish begins by remarking on the complexity of mentoring, whose felt necessity "ranges from asking for help in getting a paper published to raising impulsive or naive questions from time to time" (179). In other words, mentoring is virtually indistinguishable from the day-to-day business of teacher-student interaction—one name for which might well be mentoring.

18. Sue Rosenberg Salk, "Men in the Academy: A Psychological Profile of Harassment," in *Ivory Tower: Sexual Harassment on Campus*, ed. Michele Paludi (Albany: State University of New York Press, 1990), 143. Near the conclusion of her essay, Salk has the following sentence: "Male sexual harassers in the academy and the academy itself may well be a model institutional structure to study for an understanding of the multiple factors which promote the exploitation of women" (168–69). But if the academy itself is a factor, Salk never pauses to consider why, in the most fundamental sense, others could be as significant as this one (depending of course upon what she means by "the academy itself").

Consider in this context James Phelan's comment, apropos of his advisees: "We are not equals. For good or ill, I am the more powerful partner . . . . This inequality hangs over the way the friendship might extend outside its generative intellectual world. Many topics that friends of a different sort—people who start out more as equals—would naturally talk about remain off-limits for us. Even in cases where a lot of the usual barriers get broken down, the inequality is always there coloring things. On the whole, I find these inhibitions to be a positive thing. Without some of the barriers remaining, I might be less inclined to offer necessary negative commentary, the student less inclined to learn from it." See Phelan, *Beyond the Tenure Track: Fifteen Months in the Life of an English Professor* (Columbus: Ohio State University Press, 1991), 35.

19. Roiphe, *Morning After*, 117.

20. Mary McCarthy, *The Groves of Academe* (New York: Harcourt, Brace & World, 1951), 23. Compare the proudly demystified and public moment when Jane Gallop presents the kiss with her student: "What I mean is that we didn't just happen to be seen kissing, but we kissed like that because we knew we were being watched. And it was precisely the knowledge of being watched that made it sexy." See Gallop, *Feminist Accused*, 91.

21. Joan Blythe in "Forum: New Rules about Sex on Campus," 41.

Chapter Two

1. Paul Cantor, *The Future of Doctoral Studies in English* (New York: Modern Language Association of America, 1989), 9. But of course a discourse consists in what is said, as well as what is not. Compare Michael Bérubé, in a recent volume offered to a wider public as a collection of cutting-edge essays on academic issues. In the midst of his presentation of his own graduate education, as it reflected the usual suspects of theory, the canon, essentialism, and so on, Bérubé

makes the following statement: "I wound up writing a somewhat long dissertation, half on the academic reception of the work of Thomas Pynchon, and over the course of five years the thing became my first book, *Marginal Forces/Cultural Centers*." See Mark Edmundson, ed., *Wild Orchids and Trotsky: Messages from American Universities* (New York: Penguin Books, 1993), 187. The casualness of the phrasing seems to me quite typical of the way people refer to the writing of their dissertations, unworthy "things" in themselves, as Bérubé discloses, until reborn as books.

Hence, it almost seems an underhanded move when David Bromwich begins a discussion of George Will's political thought by producing the intelligence that he has looked up Will's Yale dissertation. "It is a massive concatenation of notes, written in a lively middle-journalistic style." See Bromwich, *Politics by Other Means: Higher Education and Group Thinking* (New Haven: Yale University Press, 1992), 58. Hence also the comedy of a dissertation so improbably having become a best-seller, a fact that continues to cause the heroine-author much embarrassment in Catherine Schine's widely-praised academic novel, *Rameau's Niece* (New York: Ticknor and Fields, 1993).

2. A composition theme, in contrast to a dissertation, neither is nor aims to be a such a writing. (Indeed, much of the burden of the composition classroom is to get students to produce *writing*, as opposed to emotional effusions, wooden pieties, and so on, all careless of grammar and organization.) Therefore, in my terms, such themes, much as they may be ridden with unwritten energies, do not have to come to terms with disguise.

On the other hand, someone who has never been able to enact, not to say write out, his sympathy with composition students does have to confront disguise. See chapter 5. Another reason why I choose the position of the student in the present chapter is because I fail to assume the position of the student in the later chapter—no matter that to a degree the composition student is structurally in the same position as the dissertating student.

3. Elizabeth Hunt, "Git 'Em Up, Move 'Em Out: The New Schemes to Push Grad Students Out Faster," *Lingua Franca* 3 (July/August 1993): 53.

4. Arguably, no decision regarding the actual writing of a dissertation is more important than this one. A dissertation is what Walter Benjamin, in "The Writer's Technique in Thirteen Theses," terms a "major work," and such work has to be planned very carefully according to its own rigors, whatever an individual's temperament. Many of Benjamin's brilliant short theses suggest that the worst way to write something major is to evaluate it chapter by chapter. I am thinking especially of the following thesis: "Talk about what you have written, by all means, but do not read from it while the work is in progress. Every gratification procured in this way will slacken your tempo. If this regime is followed, the growing desire to communicate will become in the end a motor for completion." See Walter Benjamin, "The Writer's Technique in Thirteen Theses," in *Reflections*, ed. Peter Demetz (New York: Harcourt Brace Jovanovich, 1978),

80–81. The institutionalized figure of the dissertation director, on the other hand, makes it virtually mandatory that some sort of version of this evaluation take place. A dissertation is, in a sense, all "progress."

Of course Benjamin presumes a notion of technique exclusively in terms of the writer's relationship to the material. In contrast, one reason for dissertation directors at all is so that technique can be redefined, not only in terms of tempo or stages of composition, but also in terms of authority. Less arguably, I believe, the dissertation writer's fundamental relationship is not so much with the material as with the discipline, which it is the job of the director to embody. In so doing, he or she makes exterior and explicit the politics of any writing, even the most solitary, as evoked by another of Benjamin's theses: "Let no thought pass incognito, and keep your notebook as strictly as the authorities their register of aliens."

For a less grim and more generous perspective on the politics, see James Phelan's tribute to his dissertation director, Sheldon Sacks, in *Beyond the Tenure Track: Fifteen Months in the Life of an English Professor* (Columbus: Ohio State University Press, 1991), 21–23.

5. That is, it is scarcely conceivable that any of the contributors to *Wild Orchids* could have been asked to discuss the writing of their dissertations. And yet, it must be admitted that the story of any one writing often *is* a muffled one. See, for example, Arthur Schlesinger Jr.'s foreword to Frank Bourgin, *The Great Challenge: The Myth of Laissez-Faire in the Early Republic* (New York: George Braziller, 1989), in which he examines the role of the original dissertation committee in refusing Bourgin's then-unorthodox argument forty-five years ago. (Influenced by Schlesinger's intervention, the University of Chicago belatedly granted Bourgin the Ph.D. in 1988.) Most interesting is that evidence suggests that the committee never met and that its chairman acted—if not entirely without good reason—alone.

Compare the recent account of the failed dissertation defense of Constance Benson, a Columbia University theology student. Unsurprisingly, at the center of the legal action Benson has brought against her committee is a dispute with her adviser over how often she showed him her drafts and how carefully she listened to his suggestions for revisions. See Jeffrey Goldberg, "Blindness or Insight? An Unholy Row Over Theology's De Man," *Lingua Franca* 4 (January/February 1994): 44–49. In a letter to the magazine printed in the next issue, Benson laments "abuses of power" and states as follows: "Except for committee's deliberations, oral dissertation defenses should be on the public record." See Benson, "Benson Hurts," *Lingua Franca* 4 (March/April 1994): 5.

But if defenses, why not prior conferences between candidate and director? Such questions are typical of the failure of anything to do with a dissertation director to result in a *text*. It is as if the burden of a dissertation director is to produce texts rather than to constitute any. The adviser of Margaret Nathan in Cathleen Schine's *Rameau's Niece*, for example, merits one sentence: "An aging, eminent professor who drank too much and married too many of his students, he ordered up dissertation topics as if they were dishes at an unsatisfactory restaurant, the only restaurant in town" (16).

6. This probably ought to be put more strongly: possession of a Ph.D. *is* the career. Renee Waldinger states what I take to be common wisdom, in a discussion on faculty development, with respect to a department's new members: "Whether or not the ethos of the institution that hired them stresses scholarly publications, it is in the interest of the new hires to publish since they have, after all, just finished dissertations and expect to base scholarly careers on the knowledge acquired during PhD studies." See Waldinger, "Faculty Development and Enlightened Self-Interest," *Profession* 93, 57. (*Profession* is an annual publication of the Modern Language Association.)

However, the point is sadly representative of dissertation discourse, which begins with the degree already in hand. Once more, the point about the dissertation is simply to finish it, so you can begin to have a career. But what if before you even have a dissertation topic you conceive of the career as already having begun? Compare the chapter "On Not Writing a Dissertation" in Terry Caesar, *Conspiring with Forms: Life in Academic Texts* (Athens: University of Georgia Press, 1992).

Finally, if the professional perils of not having written a dissertation need no illustration, the perils of beginning a career by publishing a first book based on a dissertation probably can never be illustrated too often. In a recent review of a book on narrative frames, for example, the reviewer fatefully finds, despite the author's standard acknowledgment that the book "had its genesis in my doctoral thesis," it "feels *so* much like a dissertation." Hence the fatal judgment: "This is apprenticeship work, a mixed stew of texts fed to a whole slew of critics." See Eric Heyne, "Transmitting the Doctoral Narrative," *Novel* 27 (Fall 1993): 119.

7. James C. Scott, *Domination and the Arts of Resistance: Hidden Transcripts* (New Haven: Yale University Press, 1990), 29.

8. Compare Alice Kaplan's story about *her* Yale dissertation director, who begins to take a personal interest when she fails to get an MLA interview in her first year on the job market. During her next, the man himself is denied tenure. One day, when Kaplan goes to the director's home to work on her conclusion, he suddenly says, "I want to go to bed with you." Kaplan sketches something of her ambivalent desire, and something of his, gives her line to him that he's out of his mind, then his to her that he's not, and simply concludes thus: "Neither of us ever mentioned it again." See Kaplan, *French Lessons: A Memoir* (Chicago: University of Chicago Press, 1993), 163. Her suggestion is that the occasion was sexual because it was textual, not vice versa.

9. So, for example, John Guillory warns against the sentiment of overthrowing the canon by changing the syllabus in the following way: "To decline the theoretical and practical labor of analyzing pedagogic structures in their institutional sites is to cede everything to the imaginary, to play the game of culture without

understanding it." See Guillory, *Cultural Capital: The Problem of Literary Canon Formation* (Chicago: University of Chicago Press, 1993), 37. A better example of a more extreme formulation would be Sande Cohen, from his chapter on "The Academic Thing": "What matters today are 'players' whose texts enable the administrative sector to thicken its image/exchange identity, the increase of value imputed directly to the academic institution itself." See Cohen, *Academia and the Luster of Capital* (Minneapolis: University of Minnesota Press, 1993), 42. In the face of such critiques, for which I have a great deal of sympathy, it seems almost banal to object, nevertheless, that the pedagogic "imaginary" can be realized with great personal force or that some players are so nimble they can arrogate to themselves more value than the institution theoretically allows.

10. For an example of the process, played out to successful conclusion, see Linda Haverty, "Getting the Job: With a Little Bit of Luck . . . and a Whole Lot of Forethought," in *The Art and Politics of College Teaching: A Practical Guide for the Beginning Professor*, ed. R. McLaren Sawyer, et al. (New York: Peter Lang, 1992), 99–114. James Phelan's *Beyond the Tenure Track* contains a candid—if insufficiently searching—account of the whole matter of how a graduate faculty member enacts the responsibility to advise students.

This responsibility is bound to become increasingly a matter of professional concern the more specific cases of sexual harassment come to light. At the conclusion of her long presentation of the recent case against Jane Gallop, Margaret Talbot reflects: "Nobody likes to talk about it much these days, but professors who spend a great deal of time and energy on particular students do not generally do so out of selfless devotion (academics are not a notably selfless lot) but out of fondness and identification or the sense that these students will reflect well on them in the wider world—what Freudians might call a libidinal investment." See Talbot, "A Most Dangerous Method," *Lingua Franca* 4 (January/February 1994): 40.

The only public argument known to me on behalf of the sexual payoff for this investment, which he denies as "defending Don Juanism," is William Kerrigan's, during a discussion of proposed bans of student-professor relationships. See "Forum: New Rules about Sex on Campus," *Harper's*, September 1993, 35–36. The same kind of payoff is everywhere suggested in Jane Gallop's recent book on being charged with sexual harassment, *Feminist Accused of Sexual Harassment* (Durham: Duke University Press, 1997), on the other hand, but nowhere actually advocated—much to the muddle of its own logic.

11. Scott, *Domination*, 14.

12. The fact that students can, and do, write about their teachers, on the other hand, often quite anecdotally and personally, indicates one way in which the authority of a teacher differs from that of a dissertation director—arguably, even in those cases where the one becomes the other for an individual. No teacher is in a position to dominate like a director, and only a teacher is subject to the phenomenon of discipleship, with its attendant erotics and dynamics of transfer-

ence, all within a broadly pedagogical, rather than a narrowly instrumental, context. On this last point, I am thinking especially of Guillory's analysis of published testimonies to Paul de Man. See *Cultural Capital*, 181–87.

A final point about suffering: it is the bedrock of Stanley Fish's remarkable presentation of professional self-hatred before the fiftieth anniversary meeting of the Harvard English Institute. Fish's point is that academics love suffering, because they love to feel oppressed before the corrupted world. It follows that they want to bestow their "rewards" to their fellows "in such a way as to render them bitter to the taste. The strategies include delay, ritual humiliations, unannounced shifts in standards, procedures that are either frustratingly secret or painfully public." See Fish, "The Unbearable Ugliness of Volvos," in *English Inside and Out: The Places of Literary Criticism*, ed. Susan Gubar and Jonathan Kamholtz (New York: Routledge, 1993), 105.

Fish doesn't mention writing a dissertation. I take it that to him the example would be too obvious—or else, perhaps, too personal insofar as his account of professional life is founded in part on his own writing experience. It seems to me (and surely to him) that he can say on this occasion things normally kept hidden, because of the sheer force of his personal authority. To cite once again the most outrageous example: "Academics like to eat shit, and in a pinch, they don't care whose shit they eat" (107). One motive for such words is to be able to exhibit the professional dominance achieved in order to be in position to utter them in the first place.

13. Scott, *Domination*, 21. Profound differences between academics-to-be and serfs must not go without saying here. One obvious difference is simply that a person can, exactly, become an academic, whereas a serf is so ascribed at birth. Whatever the subjugated fact of the woman's existence, in the above instance, before, during, and after the writing of her dissertation (she had no job when I heard the story), she was at last able to write one.

A more important qualification that needs to be made about academics can be found in Scott's later chapter on hegemony, where he argues for a "paper-thin" definition that stresses the power of subordinate groups to participate from below in social change. What about subordinate groups who come to legitimate their subordination? At least one condition must be met: the presumption of future access into the dominant class. What this means in academic terms is that even the most craven candidate who writes under the most tyrannical director knows that his or her day will come. It might turn out to mean directing a dissertation, or else forgetting about ever having had to write one.

A second condition Scott mentions to explain involuntary subordination seems to me to include more than to exclude a person writing a dissertation. Such persons are, precisely, "more or less completely atomized and kept under close observation" (83). That is, one director to each dissertation, the better to keep each candidate closely observed as well as atomized, so that no social realm can open out in which hidden or oppositional activity can develop. Indeed, the effectiveness of this very condition goes a long way in explaining why nobody subsequently writes about either dissertations or directors.

But can we expect this to continue through the '90s, when downsized administrative policies and restricted market conditions result in part-time, temporary employment, at best, for so many new Ph.D.s? If the matter of access into the dominant is so crucial, what happens to the whole representation of the very project of a dissertation when future access comes to appear illusory to so many (and present subjugation, perhaps, more clear)?

14. From the chapter "Getting along with Colleagues," Sawyer, *The Art and Politics of College Teaching*, 230. For another example of the genre, see Robert Boice, *The New Faculty Member: Supporting and Fostering Professional Development* (San Francisco: Jossey-Bass Publishers, 1992), or for a more specialized (and more blunt) presentation, Paula J. Caplan, *Lifting a Ton of Feathers: A Woman's Guide to Surviving in the Academic World* (Toronto: University of Toronto Press, 1994).

15. Cheryl Fish notes: "One kind of 'aboveboard' or clearly recognized form of academic monitoring happens when, in graduate school, a student is required to have an adviser, who directs and guides in choosing, refining, and completing a dissertation, thus paving the way for the end of the graduate career." See Fish, "'Someone to Watch Over Me': Politics and Paradoxes in Academic Monitoring," in *Working-Class Women in the Academy: Laborers in the Knowledge Factory*, ed. Michelle M. Tokarczyk and Elizabeth A. Fay (Amherst: University of Massachusetts Press, 1993), 179. Fish goes on to discuss how the process is perforce an informal one, for "there is virtually no way one can train or learn to mentor or be mentored; there is no absolute sense of what *could* or *should* be done, because of course that would vary with personality as well as with field and school" (187).

Compare *Rameau's Niece*, where the heroine's mentor figure for her second, post-dissertation manuscript, is an editor, or perhaps a dissertation director in a pastoral mode: "In a way almost unheard-of for the editor of an academic, he watched over her like a hen, clucking and fussing and proud. He admired her, protected her, manipulated her. He actually edited, too" (45). The difference is that Richard has nothing to initiate Margaret Nathan *into*, except the eternal mysteries of rewriting prose, and so she strains to keep faith that a "benefactor" can also be a "friend."

16. Tokarczyk and Fay, *Working-Class Women*, 6. Of course not so clear from the perspective of the "process" is how significant initiation into these values is deemed to be. In a sense, it is structurally important to the modern university that the initiation not be clear, and instead an example of what John Guillory would term "confused." Consider his comment on the distinction between bureaucratic and pedagogic autonomy made by Pierre Bourdieu and Jean-Claude Passeron in *Reproduction*: "It is not a question of 'lumping together' the two autonomies, when they are 'irreducible to one another,' much less of reducing

the pedagogic to the bureaucratic, but of acknowledging the overdetermination of the conception of 'autonomy' in the contemporary school." See Guillory, *Cultural Capital*, 252. The position of the dissertation director becomes one way in which autonomy is, precisely, overdetermined—and gets overdetermined according to a necessary confusion about whether this figure is supposed to teach values or administer the final phase of a degree sequence.

17. Nancy K. Miller, "Decades," in Edmundson, *Wild Orchids*, 88.

18. David Bromwich, *Politics by Other Means: Higher Education and Group Thinking* (New Haven: Yale University Press, 1992), 232. He adds that, alas, "it is still a version of the ivory tower."

The colonial model is now everywhere rife in the discursive realm, and available even to be turned back on those who benefit from it, as in an exchange in a recent *PMLA* where a professor from South Africa reminds another from Canada about "the inadequacies of the theoretical discourse that academics outside South Africa apply to this part of the world. . . . North American academics should remember," the letter continues, "that the real resources and power at their disposal are those related to the material conditions of the production of 'knowledge' in the form of scholarly publications." See Teresa Dovey, Letter, *PMLA* 110 (October 1995): 1049. Compare the invocation of this same analogy in Terry Caesar, "Theory in the Boondocks," *Yale Journal of Criticism* 6 (Fall 1993): 224.

Chapter Three

1. Quoted in Andrew Delbanco, "The Skeptical Pilgrim," *New Republic* 207 (July 6, 1992): 38.

2. I am assured that rejection forms constitute a most unusual—not to say unheard-of—procedure in Brazil, for example. Editors of academic journals make every attempt to reply personally to each contributor. Of course this is possible in a society where there are not only far fewer academics than in the United States but far fewer college graduates who might in some way aspire to authorship. I have no information on how unsolicited contributions are rejected by more popular magazines.

What degree of literacy a society might be presumed to have before it could generate some sort of normative communication regarding just about anything to do with prospective publication (outside the usual social or professional networks) is bound to be a highly speculative matter. My guess is that in the United States it is probably easier for a hopeful contributor who does not belong to any such network to get either rejected or accepted than just about any society on earth. I find it scarcely conceivable that a Brazilian would send a letter to the director of a university press such as S. S. Hanna does, providing a list of suggested responses, among them: "Enclosed is a nasty/nice letter, but don't you dare use it in any future piece for *Publishers Weekly.*" See S. S. Hanna, *The Gypsy Scholar: A Writer's Comic Search for a Publisher* (Ames: Iowa State University Press, 1987), 137. The book, an account of Hanna's attempts to get it published, details a kind of game to keep outwitting the inexorable text of rejection.

3. One major reason is because the impersonality proceeds from historical factors that foster the expression of yet more personal energies. See especially the concluding chapter, "'Personality' and the Making of Twentieth-Century Culture," in Warren Susman, *Culture as History: The Transformation of American Society in the Twentieth Century* (New York: Pantheon Books, 1983). Susman traces the development in this century from an older vision of the self founded in a concept of character to a newer vision founded on the idea of personality. Crucial to the change was the publication during the first two decades of hundreds of manuals and guides for self-improvement. "It is an almost too perfect irony," Susman notes, "that most of the works published and sold in large numbers as self-help in developing an effective personality insist that individuals should be 'themselves' and *not* follow the advice or direction of others" (277).

Just as these manuals constitute examples of a cultural text that works out some of the basic terms of a culture of personality, so do rejection forms, which attempt to efface personality. An interesting instance of the labor is provided by a recent essay in *College English* on job application replies from university English departments. The author bemoans the hopelessly impersonal consequences of the present job market, cites examples from his personal archive of five hundred rejection letters (many of which bemoan their own impersonality), and concludes thus: "My grad school adviser once told of a rejection letter he had received which began with an avuncular 'Young man, yours is a gambit which has no chance of success.' Perhaps such distinctive voices are no longer affordable in academic job rejection letters; we must, however, take care that the human voice is not lost altogether." See Ted Brown, "Unkind Cuts: Rethinking the Rhetoric of Academic Job Application Letters," *College English* 55 (November 1993): 778.

This conclusion not only ignores the standardized "gambit" the job application letter itself has become; in taking for granted the value of the individual voice, Brown fails to inquire how a vision of selfhood might be at work in the letters he mentions, notwithstanding the fact that the self, being merely "personable," is at odds with his own vision, based more on character than personality. On the rhetoric and conventions of job application letters, see the chapter "Lack of Application" in Terry Caesar, *Conspiring with Forms: Life in Academic Texts* (Athens: University of Georgia Press, 1992).

4. David Bromwich, *Politics by Other Means: Higher Education and Group Thinking* (New Haven: Yale University Press, 1992), 33. See also in the preface the citation of Eric Hobsbawm's comments on the difference between the German *Heimat* (homeland) and *Heim* (home), and the stricture in the last note to

Bromwich's final chapter on how a given community differs from a merely chosen one.

The fatuousness of academic pieties about "community" has been the subject of a number of still more recent considerations, some broadly based, in particular Russell Jacoby, *Dogmatic Wisdom: How the Culture Wars Divert Education and Distract America* (New York: Doubleday, 1994), some more inward, most especially David Damrosch, *We Scholars: Changing the Culture of the University* (Cambridge: Harvard University Press, 1995). An unusually distinguished philosophical critique of the corporatist university should also be mentioned here: Bill Readings, *The University in Ruins* (Cambridge: Harvard University Press, 1996).

5. Russell Jacoby, *The Last Intellectuals* (New York: Basic Books, 1987), 233.

6. Jack London, *Martin Eden* (New York: Penguin Books, 1985), 133.

7. Ibid., 250.

8. A trenchant review-essay, well over a decade old now, by Michael West ("Books," *College English* 41 [April 1980]) is still worth consulting. West considers a wide range of issues having to do with scholarly publication, including this particular issue of fees—rarer then than now. Submission fees, West comments, would only "exacerbate existing tensions." "In my experience," he continues, "obtuse or vacuous criticisms from referees outnumbered perceptive and helpful reports by about three to one. This situation I found irritating but quite understandable. . . . However, had I *paid* for these well-intentioned but often inept critiques, they would have enraged me." See West, "Books," 911. Requiring authors whose work has been accepted to pay charges per page would be far preferable to submission fees, West continues: "Most scholarly authors, I fancy, would part more happily with one hundred dollars for something they definitely value and get (i.e. publication) than with twenty-five dollars a crack for the privilege of being tardily rejected."

9. Paul Mariani, "Class," *New England Review* 15 (Spring 1993): 60–61.

10. Stanley Fish, *Doing What Comes Naturally* (Durham: Duke University Press, 1991), 176. The essay was originally printed in *PMLA*.

11. See Andre Bernard, ed., *Rotten Rejections: A Literary Companion* (Wainscott, N.Y.: Pushcart Press, 1990). But this small collection is almost exclusively about books, and it is often not clear whether the judgments printed were made by readers or editors. My guess is that a more comprehensive, rigorously edited compilation of readers' reports, made either for any one academic discipline or even some combination of several, could be a sensation as well as a revelation.

It would have to be judiciously edited in the case of reports on book-length manuscripts, which tend to be different in kind from reports about articles insofar as books are longer, and take longer to write. Perhaps this is why reader reports on books also tend to be more juicy and dismissive. At least I've found this to be so in my own experience. The following conclusion from a report on a collection of my travel essays is typical of the difference (if not of my own experience):

In conclusion, my opinion is that despite some strong and sometimes poetic writing . . . the author comes across in so many places as arrogant, self-centered, and racist (despite his reflexivity) that I think the value of publishing some parts of this work would be only to remind us that the Ugly American still lives, now in New Age clothing.

The expression of such an opinion would be most unusual on the reader's report of an article. Compare the most amusing few pages Gilbert Sorrentino gives of tepid editorial rejections of novels, of the "while we felt . . . we also thought" and "while we thought . . . we also felt" variety. See Sorrentino, *Mulligan Stew: A Novel* (New York: Grove Press, 1979), 82–84.

12. William D. Schaefer, *Education without Compromise: From Chaos to Coherence in Higher Education* (San Francisco: Jossey-Bass Publishers, 1990), 103.

13. Robert Lucas, *The Grants World Inside Out* (Urbana and Chicago: University of Illinois Press, 1992), 172.

14. Robert Wexelblatt, *Professors at Play* (New Brunswick: Rutgers University Press, 1991), 156–57.

15. James C. Scott, *Domination and the Arts of Resistance: Hidden Transcripts* (New Haven: Yale University Press, 1990), 3. Of course it needs hardly to be noted that, unlike most of the dominated groups Scott considers, contributors to magazines willingly enter their peculiar conditions of domination—unless one wants to argue that in the case of academics, employment itself (i.e., "publish or perish") initiates them. Elsewhere Scott remarks upon another general rule: "In principle, however, the greater the freedom of choice in entry and the greater the ease of withdrawal, the more legitimate the subordination" (82).

16. Scott, *Domination*, 15.

17. Molly Hite, *Class Porn* (Freedom, Calif.: The Crossing Press, 1987), 83. At the end of the novel she ignores her composition class, and then just dismisses it, in order to read a publisher's letter of acceptance of her "class" porn novel.

18. Editor's Column, "Scholarship, Promotion, and Tenure in Composition Studies," *College Composition and Communication* 44 (December 1993): 439.

19. Norman Maclean, "A Grudge Runs Through It," *Harper's*, February 1993, 35.

Chapter Four

1. Nancy K. Miller, "Decades," in Mark Edmundson, ed., *Wild Orchids and Trotsky: Messages from American Universities* (New York: Penguin, 1993), 94.

2. Pierre Bourdieu, *Outline of a Theory of Practice*, trans. Richard Nice (Cambridge: Cambridge University Press, 1977), 164. In the case of memos, naturalization proceeds through accumulation. Hence James Phelan writes in his journal of professional life: "I go to my mailbox, which I find stuffed with memos, notices, papers, etc., and I begin to sort through them, bringing things

that can be handled by my very capable secretary, Cartha, over to her desk, where there is also another stacking tray for me. From that I pick up more folders, memos, notes, etc., and again try to handle on the spot whatever I can." Soon students appear, and the office phone rings. The "pile" finds a place in "the already existing ecosystem." See James Phelan, *Beyond the Tenure Track: Fifteen Months in the Life of an English Professor* (Columbus: Ohio State University Press, 1991), 46–47.

3. Richard Ohmann, *English in America: A Radical View of the Profession* (New York: Oxford University Press, 1976), 191.

4. See James C. Scott, *Domination and the Arts of Resistance: Hidden Transcripts* (New Haven: Yale University Press, 1990).

5. My impression is that a business structure is typically less absorbed with matters of justification. Whether this is because of stricter notions of hierarchy in business, more fixed categories of domination and subordination, or simply greater need for results rather than reasons is difficult to say. A friend of mine who used to work for a small computer company sent me such memos as the following:

> T.SDA.LOAD library is in the process of being expanded. This process will call for the deletion of this file. The library will cease to exist after 4:30 P.M. today. This means that you will have no load modules tomorrow. All you should have to do is recompile your original source and move the text files to the library tomorrow. If this causes any one problems see me NOW.

Why is it necessary for the library to cease? The interesting thing, to an academic, is how the question is treated as an utterly technical one, with no interest at all exhibited in the necessity to expand the T.SDA.LOAD. The necessity is taken for granted. So is the tone of blunt immediacy. A department chair might write the last sentence above. But not a dean. And even a department chair, I think, would be more likely moved to express a note of regret, if not apology, at the sad loss of even a day's load modules.

6. My reference is of course to Mikhail Bakhtin's famous formulation of the "other" of literary language. See *The Dialogic Imagination: Four Essays*, ed. Michael Holquist ; trans. Caryl Emerson and Michael Holquist (Austin: University of Texas Press, 1981), 263 and *passim*. The language acceptable for the official purposes of memos (no less than literary language) exists to be continually repositioned along a hierarchy of socially marked forms of speech and writing. My point is not that the language of memos is like literary language, although, like all other language use, it can be made "literary." More simply, I mean only that the language of memos changes, if at a slower pace than heteroglossia.

7. Ohmann, *English in America*, 191. He gives the "full paradigm" of the "form of argument" embodied in *The Pentagon Papers* as follows:

1. Statement of aims

2. Analysis of the present situation, and how far the United States is from achieving its aims

3. List of possible courses of action

4. Likely advantages and disadvantages of each, in terms of the stated aims

5. Recommendation (196)

One assumes, incidentally, that the departmental archives of the Syracuse University English department would yield an especially rich trove in this connection. The department was widely reported to have been operating, not to say being administered, on the basis of memos for a number of years. See Steven Mailloux, "Rhetoric Returns to Syracuse," in *English Studies/Culture Studies: Institutionalizing Dissent*, ed. Isaiah Smithson and Nancy Ruff (Urbana: University of Illinois Press, 1994): 143–56.

8. At the other end of a textual continuum characterized by power to shape or control events, I would locate minutes. Considered strictly as a document, minutes have no authority as a textual *act* apart from confirming the meeting to which they refer. I do not mean that minutes can't be well written. What I mean instead is that this doesn't matter. Minutes are strictly transitory, "of" a specific meeting, whose actual business transpires irrespective of how the minutes are written.

In addition, meetings for which minutes constitute the only appropriate textual representation are themselves likely to be purely ephemeral, or "ongoing." At most, only occasional decisions issue from them, which are normally subject to revision through any number of other factors or groups. At the minimum, the following sort of item, from the minutes of one of my own department's meetings, appears: "There's still a problem with the coffee pot, says Carole. Lois said she will speak to the graduate students to ensure they also attend to the coffee machine."

The minutes of another meeting begin thus: "Larry announced that this meeting's main business would be the visit of Dean Scanlon. Dean Scanlon let the Department know, at 2:05, that he would be unable to join us." This did not, however, terminate a meeting that had begun five minutes earlier. The minutes record news from the Curriculum Committee and the Search Committee. Upcoming meetings of the English Club and the Writing Staff, respectively, are announced.

Finally, the chair announces that the dean's visit will be the main business of the next meeting. Minutes for a meeting such as this record, I think, a kind of zero degree of a group's relation to the future, into which the past can only be reborn as if it never occurred at all because the group has no control over "the stream of events."

9. George Greenstein, "Homi Bhabha and the Development of Modern Science," *American Scholar* 61 (Summer 1992): 415. Greenstein does not consider whether the memo he cites might not have a national text. In an otherwise fine

linguistic analysis of two memos, from National University of Singapore and United World College of South East Asia, respectively, Lester Faigley similarly fails to raise some question about how different national traditions might affect the writing of memos. About a headmaster's memo on the school dress code, Faigley has a point similar to Greenstein's: "It is as if the dress code were handed down by God, and the students are blasphemers for not following it to the letter." See Faigley, *Fragments of Rationality: Postmodernity and the Subject of Composition* (Pittsburgh: University of Pittsburgh Press, 1992), 97. Suppose we ask, however, if a paternalistic tradition is not at work in all these Asian memos, which do not issue along the lines of Westernized instrumental reason and technocratic organization.

It is quite likely, I believe, that there are some societies in which the textual practice known in the West as memo writing does not function as such. Compare Cathy N. Davidson, new to her teaching position in Japan, browsing through the accumulated memos in her mailbox, one of which (in English and Japanese) announces that "everyone should please try to have the health examination before the beginning of classes." Davidson is puzzled. "We didn't get memos at Michigan State that told us 'please try' to do things." See Davidson, 36 *Views of Mount Fuji: On Finding Myself in Japan* (New York: Dutton, 1993), 8–9.

Or else, if Western textual practice does function, in some countries memos can be shaped less like bulletins than essays. One of the best memos I have ever read was in Brazil, where the Dental School of the University of Maringa framed a response to objections about its graduation procedures by a witty allusion to Luis Bunuel's film, "The Exterminating Angel" (where only the sheep can wander in and out), and cinched the argument by citing Plutarch (about how, when Dionysius the Tyrant was going blind, the court responded by pretending to be blind as well).

10. Scott, *Domination*, 135.

11. Scott, *Domination*, 196. Of course the relation between the official structure of an organization and its social relations or other informal networks can be put in different terms to reveal the same sort of thing about bureaucratic authority. Compare Claude Lefort: "behind the mask of rules and impersonal relations lies the proliferation of unproductive functions, the play of personal contacts and the madness of authority." See Lefort, *The Political Forms of Modern Society: Bureaucracy, Democracy, Totalitarianism,* ed. John B. Thompson (Cambridge: MIT Press, 1986), 109.

12. Martha Banta, "Working the Levees: Building Them Up or Knocking Them Down?" *American Quarterly* 43 (September 1991): 383. If it could be objected that the very idea of such a course is a transparent mockery of political correctness, consider the following assertion of the same sort of thing about her course in gay literature by Eve Kosovsky Sedgwick: "I've gone so far as to include in the syllabus a request that students who consider themselves heterosexual find ways of *not* making that information available to the rest of the class until,

say, three weeks into the semester: until, that is to say, ideally, a time when they have been able to register the presumption of their queerness, not as an outlandish if educative burden, but rather precisely as—in relation to this particular cognitive and erotic space and, who knows, maybe even in relation to others—something to be explored, expanded, and prized." See Sedgwick, "Socratic Raptures, Socratic Ruptures," in *English Inside and Out. The Places of Literary Criticism*, ed. Susan Gubar and Jonathan Kamholtz (New York: Routledge, 1993), 129. What to say? Did someone speak of parody? One would certainly like to see Sedgwick's syllabus. Perhaps some ways heterosexuals could keep their mouths shut (to mention that part only) for the first three weeks are therein suggested.

13. Don DeLillo, *Americana* (New York: Pocket Books, 1973), 19.

14. Therefore, I do not quite agree with Faigley when he remarks that the sheaf of memos he received from the university "was a kind of institutional memory," containing "traditional knowledge." See Faigley, *Postmodernity*, 91. Archive would be a better word here, because the word is more neutral with respect both to the wide range of uses memos can be put to in organizations and to how all the uses finally have a purely ephemeral character—even if some memos exist to be kept on file forever.

This last use is especially true in the case of what I have earlier distinguished as position papers. But then we should attend to Robert Birnbaum's discussion of the important role in the decision-making process of "anarchical" organizations played by "garbage cans." Birnbaum writes as follows: "Garbage cans in an organization act like buffers or 'energy sinks' that absorb problems, solutions, and participants like a sponge and prevent them from sloshing around and distributing arenas in which people wish to act. Ad Hoc long-range institutional planning committees may be the quintessential garbage cans, temporarily providing 'homes' for any conceivable institutional problem, solution, or participant." See Birnbaum, *How Colleges Work: The Cybernetics of Academic Organization and Leadership* (San Francisco: Jossey-Bass, 1988), 165.

See my consideration above of the CCPS Summary, which, in Birnbaum's terms, is so much sloshing. How accurate would it be to say that the circulation of virtually all memos in any organization is ultimately a practice of waste recycling? Some of the basis for the humor of St. Augustine writing a memo is not only that he did not write as a member of an organization but that he did not write garbage.

15. Compare John Guillory's striking invocation of "the style of the memo," which he terms "the humblest text of bureaucracy," in his consideration of a key prophetic moment in Paul de Man. "It reports," he continues, "on the future *productivity* of rhetorical reading. . . . It is as though de Man were merely reporting, as though he were merely passing on instructions from somewhere higher or deeper within the institution itself, and not setting an agenda for his disciples, for the school (and faction) of rhetorical reading." De Man, in other

words, has chosen a familiar "style" best suited to concealing, like a good bureaucrat, the presence of his own charismatic authority. See Guillory, *Cultural Capital: The Problem of Literary Canon Formation* (Chicago: University of Chicago Press, 1993), 258–59.

It might well be possible to stipulate a sort of zero-degree function of the memo, although even here function depends upon reception. Russell Jacoby recalls a controversy that swelled to national proportions a few years ago when A. Bartlett Giamatti issued the following memo on his first day as president of Yale:

> In order to repair what Milton called the ruin of our grandparents, I wish to announce that henceforth, as a matter of University policy, evil is abolished and paradise restored. I trust all of us will do whatever is possible to achieve this policy objective.

See Jacoby, *Dogmatic Wisdom: How the Culture Wars Divert Education and Distract America* (New York: Doubleday, 1994), 23. The reasons for the controversy are complex. The theoretical questions interest me most, including whether a memo must be limited to its specific institutional or organizational setting in order to function officially. Giamatti's memo raises a still more provocative question: can a memo mock its own authority and still be a memo? Certainly some of the controversy expresses outrage at the spectacle of a college president mocking his own authority, and, perhaps worse, doing so by means of one of the culture's most revered textual forms.

16. Compare Scott on the "undominated discourse" of the Bakhtinian carnivalesque (through Rabelais), "where there was no servility, false pretenses, obsequiousness, or etiquettes of circumlocution." See *Domination*, 175. Scott goes on to criticize this notion of carnival speech as being too ideal. No speech escapes the power relations in which it must be enunciated and measured. My own point is that parody speech within an academic context is highly strategic, and based on accepting its restraints, if not the communicative dynamics of the context itself.

17. Scott, *Domination*, 206.

18. Susan Horton, "Let's Get 'Literate': English Department Politics and a Proposal for a Ph.D. in Literacy," in *Pedagogy Is Politics: Literary Theory and Critical Teaching*, ed. Maria-Regina Kecht (Urbana: University of Illinois Press, 1993), 135.

Compare Jane Gallop: "Once sexual harassment is detached from its feminist meanings, it becomes possible to imagine feminism itself accused as a form of sexual harassment." See Gallop, *Feminist Accused of Sexual Harassment* (Durham: Duke University Press, 1997), 29. In other words, far from forgetting, Gallop's idea of a reinvigorated decorous talk flaunts the "disease," as she goes on to argue.

19. Jacoby, *Dogmatic Wisdom*, 91.

20. Paul Theroux, *The London Embassy* (Boston: Houghton Mifflin Company, 1983), 246.

Chapter Five

1. Jane Gallop, "Knot a Love Story," *Yale Review of Criticism* 5 (Fall 1992): 209. David Lodge's celebrated aviational fiction about academics, *Small World* (New York: Macmillan, 1984), is of course about conferences, not classes. The narrative's prize, the UNESCO Chair of Literary Criticism, carries with it no teaching duties at all, and is unconnected with any particular institution or country.

2. Stephen Greenblatt's study of New World exploration, for example, manages to restrict this moment in his acknowledgments to one student. The student is unnamed. She asked a question after one of his lectures that enables Greenblatt to give a sharper account of his own relation to his materials—and, now, to his readers. See Greenblatt, *Marvelous Possessions: The Wonder of the New World* (Chicago: University of Chicago Press, 1991), viii–ix. Greenblatt has already recorded his impressive debts to some ninety individually named people, encompassing no less than five countries.

3. It is mentioned in another essay I did manage to publish about the actual circumstances of teaching another survey course. See Terry Caesar, "Pieties and Theories: The Heath in the Survey, the Survey in the Discipline," *Arizona Quarterly* 51 (Winter 1995): 109–40. For more on the lowly status of a survey course in any curriculum or discipline (not to say the mere teacher—as opposed to scholar—usually responsible for such a course), see David Damrosch, *We Scholars: Changing the Culture of the University* (Cambridge: Harvard University Press, 1995).

4. Evan Watkins, *Work Time: English Departments and the Circulation of Cultural Value* (Palo Alto: Stanford University Press, 1989), 218. He continues: "Teaching in contrast merely circulates in the classroom what has already been made available in one form or another in publication. That is, the link articulating the translation from one economy to the other is *repetition*." But already I believe Watkins is reinstituting his own version of a binary which the actual conditions at major research universities unsettle, if only by casting teaching in the form of research.

For another example of how difficult it is for professors from such universities so much as to imagine conducting a discussion in nonprivileged terms, see Russell Jacoby's comments on Gerald Graff's *Beyond the Culture Wars* in *Dogmatic Wisdom: How the Culture Wars Divert Education and Distract America* (New York: Doubleday, 1994), 184–88. A recent review by Margery Sabin marks the same failure by noting that "Graff skips over the crucial point that what might be called the 'literary' side of his imagined debate requires training in the skills of attention and thought that are not currently regarded as intellectually interesting in the most prestigious graduate programs." See Sabin, "'The Debate': Seductions and Betrayals in Literary Studies," *Raritan* 8 (Winter 1994): 128. Teaching exclusively in such programs, it appears, can only lead to arguments that wave aside very different teaching circumstances in which the need for enduring "pieties" is as essential as the need for new research.

5. Frank Lentricchia, *The Edge of Night* (New York: Random House, 1994), 181. Compare the far more protracted account of teaching by the far less imperious James Phelan, *Beyond the Tenure Track: Fifteen Months in the Life of an English Professor* (Columbus: Ohio State University Press, 1991). The climax of the book, nonetheless, is when Phelan learns his next book has been accepted — the book he has already been teaching to graduate students, on the basis of his last one.

No wonder his response when, on a recruiting trip for minority students, Phelan meets a woman at Corpus Christi State. "She has no free time," he writes, "very little money, and endless responsibilities to students, conditions which make it virtually impossible for her to publish." Phelan concludes thus: "Our conversation made me feel that my job is a sinecure" (69). Lentricchia, it might be finally noted, goes into an abbey rather than on a recruiting trip.

6. James C. Scott, *Domination and the Arts of Resistance: Hidden Transcripts* (New Haven: Yale University Press, 1990), 4.

7. The following statement by David Bromwich cannot be emphasized enough: "The guiding concern and solicitude of the academic system are felt to be obligatory in exact proportion to the absence of such helps in the organized system outside." See Bromwich, *Politics by Other Means: Higher Education and Group Thinking* (New Haven: Yale University Press, 1992), 30.

8. Dean Whitla, "The Making of a Scholarly Career at a Major Research University," in *The Art and Politics of College Teaching: A Practical Guide for the Beginning Professor*, ed. R. McLaran Sawyer, Keith W. Prichard, and Karl D. Hostetler (New York: Peter Lang, 1992), 17.

9. Gallop, "Knot a Love Story," 213. Compare the following comment from the introduction to her latest book: "This book, which took too long to write, not only passes through two different theoretical formations but around 1989 begins to feel the pressure of a third and grows increasingly anxious as I push to get it done and out before its power of strategic intervention is lost, before it enters a configuration different than the one for/in which it was written." See Jane Gallop, *Around 1981: Academic Feminist Literary Theory* (New York: Routledge, 1992), 4. Gallop doesn't stay to say why the book took too long to write. Could one reason be because it took too long to teach? In any case, a better statement could scarcely be imagined about the ongoing crisis of producing the new while doing the same old thing.

Under the circumstances, life is bound to become more than a little confusing, unless one is careful. Apparently Gallop hasn't been as a teacher. See the account of the sexual harassment charges brought against her in Margaret Talbot, "A Most Dangerous Method," *Lingua Franca* 4 (January/February 1994): 1, 24–40.

10. Edward Allen, *Mustang Sally* (New York: W. W. Norton & Company, 1993), 187. Allen's hero comments as follows: "I feel as if I should hate all this stuff, but I don't. They're sincere. They're stupid, but they don't want to hurt anybody. Even the poor Auschwitz kids, with their parents' rage echoing in their heads: they just want things to be easy." See also the list of Instructor's Guides and Directed Worksheets on 184–85, and especially the wonderful parody of a lengthy composition, entitled "Things Happen in Pairs of Threes," on 30–37. On my own appreciation of the student text in composition, see *Conspiring with Forms: Life in Academic Texts* (Athens: University of Georgia Press, 1992). For a more extended novelistic presentation of the witless terrors of teaching this text, see Molly Hite, *Class Porn* (Freedom, Calif.: The Crossing Press, 1987).

11. Eve Kosofsky Sedgwick, "Queer and Now," in *Wild Orchids and Trotsky: Messages from American Universities*, ed. Mark Edmundson (New York: Penguin Books, 1993), 243.

12. Pam Annas, "Pass the Cake: The Politics of Gender, Class, and Text in the Academic Workplace," in *Working-Class Women in the Academy: Laborers in the Knowledge Factory*, ed. Michelle M. Tokarczyk and Elizabeth A. Fay (Amherst: University of Massachusetts Press, 1993), 175.

13. Laura Weaver, "A Mennonite 'Hard Worker' Moves from the Working Class and the Religious/Ethnic Community to the Academy: A Conflict between Two Definitions of 'Work,'" in Tokarczyk and Fay, 121. Some perspective on both smile and strategy is provided by Stanley Fish's address to the English Institute, in which he makes the central point that academics want to complain, and then continues as follows: "The reason that academics want and need their complaints is that it is important for them to feel oppressed, for in the psychic economy of the academy, oppression is the sign of virtue. The more victimized you are, the more subject to various forms of humiliation, the more you can tell yourself that you are in the proper relation to the corrupted judgment of mere worldly eyes." See Fish, "The Unbearable Ugliness of Volvos," in *English Inside and Out: The Places of Literary Criticism*, ed. Susan Gubar and Jonathan Kamholtz (New York: Routledge, 1993), 105.

But Fish gets a couple of things wrong. The superior victimization of composition teachers ought to count for as much in the academy as it does outside it. It doesn't; see Hite's novel, *Class Porn*, or almost any serious discussion of teaching in the '90s, which necessarily includes the plight (as well as the consequences) of so many part-time, temporary teachers, who, in English, almost exclusively are underpaid to teach composition. Within the academy it makes an enormous difference if you complain about having to meet deadlines for publication rather than for grading themes or examinations.

14. Discussing the difference between standard and literary language within the context of canonicity, John Guillory argues that the expansion of composition at the university level discloses "a failure to install the standard vernacular at lower levels of the educational system." He continues: "The disintegration of the standard also throws into relief the institutional interdependence of composition and literature, widely misrecognized as a disrelation." See Guillory, *Cultural Capital: The Problem of Literary Canon Formation* (Chicago: University of Chicago Press, 1993), 79. This is indeed a complicated question. Here I think Guillory himself misrecognizes an institutional relation, which is political, for a disciplinary one, which is theoretical. Of course he could well reply that the inextricability of the one question from the other is the essence of the complication.

How closely related composition and literature are is not a widely debated issue from the literary side. Guillory's critique is incisive concerning why. The text of composition, he writes, is concerned with the speech of the professional-managerial class. "The point of greatest historical interest about this speech is that its production bypasses the older literary syllabus altogether. Students need no longer immerse themselves in that body of writing called 'literature' in order to acquire 'literary' language" (79–80). To the degree that composition either actively appropriates or is in a structural position to appropriate the power of literary language, literature must, I think, disassociate itself from composition, even if hands-across-the-disciplines are extended from either direction over a mutual interest in rhetoric.

For an illustration of how this hopeless theoretical division plays itself out on one campus, see Jacoby's sketch of the teaching of the expository writing course at the University of Texas, in *Dogmatic Wisdom*, 105–6. The course comes value-added, or, depending upon one's point of view, extracted: instructors are forbidden to use literature.

15. Lisa Ede, "On Writing Reading and Reading Writing," in *Encountering Student Texts: Interpretive Issues in Reading Student Writing*, ed. Bruce Lawson, Susan Sterr Ryan, and W. Ross Winterowd (Urbana: National Council of Teachers of English, 1989), 152.

16. An excellent place to begin is provided by many of the contributions to Richard H. Bullock and John Trimbur, eds., *The Politics of Writing Instruction: Postsecondary* (Portsmouth, N.H.: Boynton/Cook Publishers, 1991). I would especially recommend the essays by James Berlin and Bruce Herzberg, although virtually all are unusually alert to the inequities and curiosities of how composition continues to be situated in English departments. I don't believe, however, that composition theorists are ultimately adequate to what Reed Way Dasenbrock, reviewing a new book by Peter Elbow, identifies as the confusion between "the teaching of writing—which is indeed 'downtrodden'—and the study of writing as an academic field. The ostensible fight over the last generation has been about the former, but the only victories have been in the latter." See

Dasenbrock, "Review: What is English Anyway?" *College English* 55 (September 1993): 546. Indeed, this confusion seems to me so central it may well be constitutive of the very field of the study of writing as an academic field.

17. Sedgwick, "Queer and Now," in Edmundson, 262–63. But compare Guillory, in a brilliant chapter on Paul de Man, and the theoretical "superstar" phenomenon of the 1980s: "The social horizon circumscribing and conditioning the emergence of the academic superstar is thus nothing less than the total socioeconomic order, within which the pervasive mass-cultural form of the celebrity system is directly (but at the same time invisibly) correlated to the disappearance of 'work autonomy' at every level and in every sphere of the workforce." See Guillory, *Cultural Capital*, 255. See also David Shumway, "The Star System in Literary Studies," *PMLA* 112 (January 1997): 85–100.

18. Gerald Graff, *Beyond the Culture Wars: How Teaching the Conflicts Can Revitalize American Education* (New York: W. W. Norton & Company, 1992), 114. For an example of how permeable the structure can be at Duke, see Jane Tompkins's account, "Let's Get Lost," in *Confessions of the Critics*, ed. H. Aram Veeser (New York: Routledge, 1996). Tompkins details the activities involved in her course, American Literature Unbound, which included a trip to a barrier island off the North Carolina coast and to a slave plantation, in conjunction with reading *Moby Dick* and Toni Morrison's *Beloved*, respectively. It might be noted that even here there was a potential writing (as if confirmed by the subsequent publication of this account), which Tompkins anticipates as follows: "The deep text was my own need to be accepted by the students. To be part of something they were part of. Not to be alone" (270).

19. Valerie Miner, "Writing and Teaching with Class," in Tokarczyk and Fay, 81.

20. "Class Discussion: A Dialogue between Kate Ellis and Lillian Robinson," in Tokarczyk and Fay, 45.

21. Michelle Tokarczyk, "By the Rivers of Babylon," in Tokarczyk and Fay, 317.

22. Evan Watkins, "Intellectual Work and Pedagogical Circulation in English," in *Theory/Pedagogy/Politics: Texts for Change*, ed. Donald Morton and Masud Zavarzadeh (Urbana: University of Illinois Press), 214. Watkins makes this comment in the context of a proposal for at once reorganizing the nature of published material and recirculating it at various levels of worksites in English throughout the country. What he wants is an "apparatus whose *use* was less to present original research than to connect the pedagogical effects of work." Although the circulation of professional publication in Brazil resembles his proposal in a very fragmented way at best, my impression is that what is published tends to be, exactly in Watkins's sense, useful to Brazilian professors.

For his full analysis of how original research changes the nature of academic work, see *Work Time*—everywhere, but especially 164 (on how concrete labor is "defeated" by the predations of abstract labor forces) and 236–37 (for an argument on how concrete labor seeks to renew itself as free through the "idealization" of the new). See also the critique of James Phelan in Jeffrey Williams, "The Life of the Mind and the Academic Situation," *College Literature* 23 (October 1996): 128–46.

23. This feeling is a staple of the occasional accounts of living abroad written by professors. For example, Cathy Davidson is given courses in oral English to teach at Kansai Women's University—a subject not, presumably, part of her regular teaching load at Michigan State. Apparently she enjoys the experience (in no small part because it enables her to practice her Japanese as well as learn about Japan). Her comments about her own role at the conclusion of the single chapter devoted to teaching are inconclusive. "At my most cynical," Davidson writes, "I think of myself as a diversion, a respite from frenetic Japanese life, the pedagogical equivalent of the *sarariiman's* whiskey. . . . When I'm feeling optimistic, I like to think I give my Japanese students the same thing I try to give my American students back home: a space in which to speak and be heard." See Davidson, 36 *Views of Mount Fuji: On Finding Myself in Japan* (New York: Dutton, 1993), 59.

24. Phelan, *Beyond the Tenure Track*, 217. The notion of "place" here is at once so figurative in the generalized sense he intends and so personal in the literal sense he does not intend that we must simply forget an earlier moment in the book. Thinking of how different life might have been if he had been Berkeley's first rather than second choice, Phelan concludes that such "idle speculation" functions for him as a reminder of "how so many academics don't have much choice about some of the basic conditions of their lives—especially where to live" (61).

25. Daniel O'Hara, *Radical Parody: American Culture and Critical Agency after Foucault* (New York: Columbia University Press, 1992), 251. O'Hara continues still further about "critical identity formation": "As such critical identity is necessarily and radically socialized, indeed inescapably if internally political, fundamentally dynamic, self-consciously erotic, and so, almost by definition, constitutionally ironic." Some of the irony is that O'Hara is now reading Lentricchia, as he acknowledges in his notes, from a manuscript copy not yet in the public domain. Perhaps, though, this is itself an example of how radically socialized a critical identity—if not a critical discourse—can become.

At the time of his writing, O'Hara did not have available all of the pages that became *The Edge of Night*, including the last, where Lentricchia cites his father exclaiming to him over the fakery of a Hollywood studio the two once toured together (182). I read this conclusion to disclose an irony so constitutive it may no longer amount of an identity. In O'Hara's terms, I am not certain whether such a reading would be edifying or merely postmodern.

For another sovereign practice, see Gayatri Chakravorty Spivak, *Outside in the Teaching Machine* (New York: Routledge, 1993). Spivak, I believe, does not mean her title to be ironic. She refers rather proudly, for example, to her "persistent critique" as "Outside in every machine" (14). Perhaps we are to read the adjective in her title as the name of a rather hapless, remorseless trope, although Spivak is in fact so "outside" teaching in any vulgar experiential sense that she loftily gestures at merely one specific pedagogical proposal in the whole book: doctoral students in English should be required to study in another language (275–76).

Chapter 6

1. See Paul Lauter's chapter, "A Scandalous Misuse of Faculty-Adjuncts," in his *Canons and Contexts* (New York: Oxford University Press, 1991). I do not see how Lauter's analysis can be bettered, although an even wider context is provided by Stanley Aronowitz and William DiFazio, *The Jobless Future: Sci-Tech and the Dogma of Work* (Minneapolis: University of Minnesota Press, 1994). As Lauter states: "the spread of adjunct employment is no rationally correctable error, but, on the contrary, a function of hard, institutional, class-conscious calculation" (206).

Alas, however, Lauter says nothing about the relation between this employment practice and tenure. Nor does James Phelan in *Beyond the Tenure Track: Fifteen Months in the Life of an English Professor* (Columbus: Ohio State University Press, 1991). But Phelan may be recommended for stray intelligence on the general matter of institutional and professional expectations after tenure, especially concerning research and publication (e.g., 12–14). For a passionate recent defense of tenure which does register the presence of adjunct employment, see Annette Kolodny, "'60 Minutes' at the University of Arizona: The Polemic against Tenure," *New Literary History* 27 (Autumn 1996): 679–704.

2. Jacob Neusner, "What It Takes for Professors to Get Themselves Fired," *Chronicle of Higher Education*, March 17, 1993, A52.

3. Cathy N. Davidson, *36 Views of Mount Fuji: On Finding Myself in Japan* (New York: Dutton, 1993), 205. This sentence might be offered as the most professionally unselfconscious one written by an American academic in a number of years. If Davidson imagines she has any part-time or temporary colleagues as readers, she does not indicate it. Of course, one could say that she cannot imagine such readers because she has virtually nothing to do with such colleagues, which is exactly the "calculated" state of affairs Lauter is talking about.

The sheer amount of *movement* among faculty at American universities constitutes an enormous and, to my knowledge, almost completely unexplored field of research. Just to restrict it: how many academics resign from their positions each year? Have numbers changed over the past decade? See the case of a University of Texas English professor, who resigned and "fled" to a "smaller" school, according to Russell Jacoby in *Dogmatic Wisdom: How the Culture Wars Divert Education and Distract America* (New York: Doubleday, 1994), 37–38. Jacoby cites local newspaper accounts.

Presumably he contacted Goddard College directly concerning another case where a faculty member was reportedly fired. Goddard reports no one by that name since 1938. Jacoby allows that the man may have been "a part-time, adjunct or extension instructor whom the college barely knew existed" (39). Such people, with scarcely enough presence from which to absent themselves, comprise a kind of black hole of academic employment, and it seems to me as little is known about their vanishing as is known about the precise conditions that enable suns to shine in other galaxies.

4. Charles Altieri, "What is At Stake in Confessional Criticism," in *Confessions of the Critics*, ed. H. Aram Veeser (New York: Routledge, 1996), 57–58. For two examples of such stories, see Mark Johnson, "Professions beyond the Academy" and Alison Smith, "Secondary Education: Still an Ignored Market," in the magazine put out once a year by the Modern Language Association, *Profession* 96, 60–68 and 69–72, respectively. Each of these pieces provides a narrative of success (i.e., each author has a job—Johnson in technical writing, Smith in high school) and therefore both are short on autobiography to the degree they are long on theoretical casehood. As such, each contributes to a rewriting of the public transcript for the downsized '90s in higher education, as opposed to the hidden transcript, in which jobs are almost impossible to come by and experience fairly begs representational means. For example, I suggest to a former student, finishing his dissertation on William S. Burroughs while working in a cafe, that he might consider retooling his subject in order to apply for Writing Center positions, which still seem to exist. He responds with some thoughts on how his dissertation could be retitled: "An Alternative to Grading: WSB's Cut-Up as Evaluative Model" or "A Gallows in My Office and a 9mm at My Hip: WSB and the 'Problem Student.'" Months ago he gave up on trying to write about the blithe indifference of his dissertation director, and I've given up urging him to withstand the blows of rejection letters that submitted articles are heir to.

5. Samuel Pickering, Jr., "Good-bye Dartmouth, or Thirty-five, Fat, Slow, and Unemployed," *College English* 39 (March 1978): 849. Compare from another twenty years previous to this, an essay that used to be in many anthologies of reading for composition classes, Herbert Gold's "A Dog in Brooklyn, A Girl in Detroit: Life among the Humanities," available in *Harbrace College Reader*, ed. Mark Schorer, et al. (New York: Harcourt, Brace & World, 1964). After detailing his sad pedagogical story, Gold concludes as follows: "It would be oversimplifying to say that I left off teaching Humanities merely because of such an experience. . . . I also left for fitter jobs, more money, a different life" (262).

6. Consider, for example, Eve Kosofsky Sedgwick, who explains to an interviewer: "There are important senses in which 'queer' can signify only when attached to the first person." See Adam Begley, "The I's Have It: Duke's '*Moi*'

Critics Expose Themselves, 4 (March/April 1994): 57. Whether or not having breast cancer is one of those senses, we can be fairly certain that Sedgwick herself would hardly admit that having an endowed chair at Duke is not one of those senses. Her academic position is too inward. She wants, instead, to get out and stay out—and damn the relation between remaining secure and performing queer, or between an extravagant critical identity and a commonplace one that either has no security or too much.

The subject of breast cancer begins Sedgwick's remarkable performance "Socratic Raptures, Socratic Ruptures: Notes toward Queer Performativity," in *English Inside and Out: The Places of Literary Criticism*, ed. Susan Gubar and Jonathan Kamholtz (New York: Routledge, 1993), and reprinted in *Tendencies* (Durham: Duke University Press, 1993). The subject of others appears in another interview, in which Sedgwick states as follows: "You learn a lot from the experiment of having a public-private persona, edging its way through ideas and issues. That would be hard to give up, but it would be completely counter-productive for all of that to result chiefly in the magnification of a particular person. It's only a meaningful project to the extent that it invites and incites and empowers and makes new kinds of space for other people who have some important uses to make of it." See Jeffrey Williams, "Sedgwick Unplugged," *Minnesota Review*, n.s., 40 (Spring/Summer 1993): 62-63.

7. Paula J. Caplan, *Lifting a Ton of Feathers: A Woman's Guide to Surviving in the Academic World* (Toronto: University of Toronto Press, 1993), 82.

8. Altieri, "What Is at Stake," 57. Compare a more forceful way of urging the same point: "The low-Other is despised and denied at the level of political organization and social being whilst it is instrumentally constitutive of the shared imaginary repertoires of the dominant culture." See Peter Stallybrass and Allon White, *The Politics and Poetics of Transgression* (Ithaca: Cornell University Press, 1986), 5-6.

9. Compare Daniel O'Hara, on the unfortunate celebration of "sublime, professionally self-serving individual mask-play in the grand Emersonian tradition." He continues about those who rhapsodize such practice: "Their self-subverting peans to the self-made individual appear, ironically enough, precisely when they are most loudly proclaiming their devoted engagement with grander issues." See O'Hara, *Radical Parody: American Culture and Critical Agency after Foucault* (New York: Columbia University Press, 1992), x. The book does not mention Sedgwick, although it does conclude with a pean to her Duke colleague, Frank Lentricchia, who, it would appear, can be commended in her place because of his superior irony.

10. Sedgwick, "Socratic Raptures, Socratic Ruptures," 132.

11. James C. Scott, *Domination and the Arts of Resistance: Hidden Transcripts* (New Haven: Yale University Press, 1990), 9.

12. Homi Bhabha, "The World and the Home," *Social Text* 31/32 (1992): 145-46. See also Homi Bhabha, "Of Mimicry and Man: the Ambivalence of Colo-

nial Discourse," *October* 28 (Spring 1984): 125-33, and Gayatri Chakravorty Spivak, *The Post-Colonial Critic: Interviews, Strategies, Dialogues* (New York: Routledge, 1990).

13. After a concluding paragraph conceding a number of features that alone make the house different than it would be in Japan (an earlier passage notes that the apartments she and her husband saw in Japan typically included Western as well as Japanese furniture), Davidson states as follows: "Maybe that's the whole point. Kyoto is a long, long way from Cedar Grove, although sometimes it feels next door." See *36 Views*, 287.

James Clifford has a fine, searching treatment of the provocations and undecidabilities of modern travel in which he begins within the anthropological project by rebuking the perpetual notion of fieldwork as "a special kind of localized *dwelling.*" See Clifford, "Traveling Cultures," in *Cultural Studies*, ed. Lawrence Grossberg, Cary Nelson, and Paula Treichler (New York: Routledge, 1992), 98. The sort of teaching Davidson does might be phrased as a special kind of globalized re-dwelling. Later, Clifford speaks the fact that "many different kinds of people travel, acquiring complex knowledges, stories, political and intercultural understandings, without producing 'travel writing'" (107). Indeed. Davidson's travel is very different than the international conferencing fictionally recreated in David Lodge's *Small World* (New York: Macmillan, 1984), where hardly anybody among the dedicated, ambitious professionals so much as gets away from this week's grand hotel or conference center.

Davidson instead writes a travel book—comparable in its way to recent accounts of localized dwelling by professional travel writers such as Jonathan Raban. (See *Hunting Mister Heartbreak: A Discovery of America* [New York: HarperCollins, 1991].) Nonetheless, she writes as an academic. An academic does not have the same relation to those who stay at home as a travel writer does, and therefore I believe she is the more pointedly accountable to the following strictures Clifford makes about dominant travel discourse, still anchored in Victorian bourgeois experience: "A host of servants, helpers, companions, guides, bearers etc. have been discursively excluded from the role of proper travelers because of their race and class, and because theirs seemed to be a dependent status in relation to the supposed independence of the individualistic, bourgeois voyager" (106).

14. Kwame Anthony Appiah and Henry Louis Gates, Jr., "Editors' Introduction: Multiplying Identities," *Critical Inquiry* 18 (Summer 1992): 628.

15. Gayatri Chakravorty Spivak, "Acting Bits/Identity Talk," *Critical Inquiry* 18 (Summer 1992): 779. "What we call experience," she later remarks, "is a staging of experience, sometimes on the small screen" (781). For the most part, although the essay is studded with "personalistic" as well as lofty asides, Spivak mounts her experience on the big screen. One would not be surprised, however, to see her critical theory as cultural politics make the same move into "another intensity" represented by the personal essay that Frank Lentricchia does, according to

Daniel O'Hara's discussion of his "sublime" trajectory in *Radical Parody*, 269. Indeed, as I suggest, "Acting Bits/Identity Bits" *is* a personal essay in disguise, quite locatable in the terms discussed by G. Douglas Atkins, *Estranging the Familiar: Toward a Revitalized Critical Writing* (Athens: University of Georgia Press, 1992). The degree of Spivak's own discomfort with this awareness may be assessed by considering her latest—and perhaps most fully autobiographical—staging, "Lives," in Veeser, *Confessions*, 205-20.

16. Another research project: how many faculty members at American universities either hold passports from other countries or are naturalized U.S. citizens? At one point in a superb treatment of general education, Michael Geyer remarks of its "multitrack" purposes: "This pluralist multiculturalism uses women, minorities, and the world's cultures (and a fictious, elevated reading of their texts) in order to reproduce what 'American' culture, thoroughly commercialized as it is, does not maintain on its own." See Geyer, "Multiculturalism and the Politics of General Education," *Critical Inquiry* 19 (Spring 1993): 516. My point is that this larger appropriation includes within it not only the travel abroad of Americans who teach in the United States but of others who come to the U.S. to teach. It is not merely a question of their identities. Their travel, remarkably varied in itself, has no status or power to destabilize what Geyer terms "the fiction of autonomy." This is the same spurious autonomy, in turn, saluted by, of all people, Edward Said (who should know better from his own national-institutional context) at the end of his essay, "Identity, Authority, and Freedom," in *The Future of Academic Freedom*, ed. Louis Menand (Chicago: University of Chicago Press, 1986): 214–28.

17. John Sutherland, "It's a Battlefield," *Times Literary Supplement*, May 28, 1993.

18. Mary McCarthy, *The Groves of Academe* (New York: Harcourt Brace & World, 1951), 151. Hereafter cited in parentheses.

19. Donald Hall, *Life Work* (Boston: Beacon Press, 1993), 4.

20. James Phelan, *Beyond the Tenure Track*, 218.

21. Charles Altieri, *Canons and Consequences: Reflections on the Ethical Force of Imaginative Ideals* (Evanston: Northwestern University Press, 1990), 208.

Index

A Note about the Author

Terry Caesar is professor of English at Clarion University. He is the author of a previous book on academic life, *Conspiring with Forms* (University of Georgia Press, 1992), as well as a study of American travel writing, *Forgiving the Boundaries* (Georgia, 1995).